Politics in Minnesota

POLITICS IN MINNESOTA

G. Theodore Mitau

CHANCELLOR, MINNESOTA STATE COLLEGE SYSTEM,
AND ADJUNCT PROFESSOR OF POLITICAL SCIENCE,
MACALESTER COLLEGE

second revised edition

University of Minnesota Press, **MINNEAPOLIS**

Printed in the United States of America at the
Jones Press, Inc., Minneapolis

Library of Congress Catalog Card Number: 78-110660

PUBLISHED IN GREAT BRITAIN, INDIA, AND PAKISTAN BY THE
OXFORD UNIVERSITY PRESS, LONDON, BOMBAY, AND KARACHI
AND IN CANADA BY THE COPP CLARK PUBLISHING CO.
LIMITED, TORONTO

ISBN: 0-8166-0558-0

FOREWORD TO THE FIRST EDITION

THERE must be many citizens of Minnesota and many political observers elsewhere who have long felt the need for just such a book as this — a brief, systematic, reliable, and up-to-date account of politics in Minnesota. It provides information and insights to be found in no other book now available. Recent and contemporary political leaders like John A. Johnson, Theodore Christianson, Floyd B. Olson, Harold E. Stassen, Luther W. Youngdahl, Hubert H. Humphrey, and Orville L. Freeman march by in brief review, while the Republican and Democratic parties, the Nonpartisan League, the Democratic-Farmer-Labor party, and minor political groups and movements (even to the Communists), with their varied ups and downs and transformations, make up an ever-living, ever-changing background. There are substantial and informative chapters on current political problems, also — on the state's election laws and party organizations, on the "nonpartisan partisan legislature," and on lobbying before the legislature. The supplementary materials at the end of the volume contain in easy reference form highly interesting and useful information, both biographical and statistical.

The author has qualified himself for the writing of this book by long study and the preparation of special articles in the field. He has in fact made himself an important authority on Minnesota politics. His style is necessarily compact, to say so much in so little space, but at the same time it is clear, flexible, and interesting.

It is my hope that this book will have a wide reading. No one can understand the government and politics of the United States as a whole, or be an effective citizen in national, state, or local affairs, without knowing a great deal about politics in his own and other states.

Let us hope that this book will be followed by another in which the actual organization and workings of state and local government in Minnesota are set forth, and the great issues of public policy are discussed. I refer, of course, to state and local administrative organization, the judicial system, the state and local services, budgeting and finance, the interrelations of state and local governments, and the operation of the process of popular government as a whole. These call for another book.

In the meantime, we owe thanks to the author of this one for a fine start along the road to greater political understanding.

WILLIAM ANDERSON
University of Minnesota

February 1960

CONTENTS

CONTENTS

Politics in Minnesota

1

PARTY PATTERNS, ISSUES, AND LEADERS

CONSERVATIVE in its governmental institutions, often liberal and sometimes radical in its politics, Minnesota offers a fascinating study in contrasts.

The state's constitution is one of the oldest in the nation: in fundamental principle and framework it is today the same charter that was ratified by Congress in 1858 when Minnesota entered the Union as the thirty-second state. It has been amended 93 times — but a majority of all constitutional changes submitted to the voters since 1900 have been rejected, and periodic proposals for a thoroughgoing revision through a new constitutional convention have been unsuccessful.

The government of the state has the traditional division of powers among executive, judicial, and legislative branches. (Its one unusual aspect is the officially "nonpartisan" character of the legislature — since 1913 state senators and representatives have been elected on a ballot that does not identify candidates by party label.) Only slowly has the machinery of state government been modified to accommodate changes in the lives of its citizens as Minnesota developed from the near-frontier, largely rural economy of the late 1850's, when the population was 150,000, to the complex modern society and more than 3 million population at the end of the 1960's. The regular term of the legislature, for example, was in 1961 still that established in 1887 — 90 days every two years — although legislative business had increased severalfold in the interim. And the districts in which legislators ran for office were the same in the 1960 election as in 1912, despite large shifts in population from district

3

to district over the years. To some degree change has been accomplished in all three branches — the legislative session was lengthened to 120 days in 1962, and new legislative districts were drawn for the 1962 election and again for 1966 — but the pace has been deliberate.

Yet, while reluctant to make innovations in the state's basic governmental structure, Minnesotans have not hesitated to experiment politically whenever their needs were not being met. When farm prices dropped, when credit was tight, when thousands were unemployed, the state's discontented swelled the ranks of third parties that challenged the power of corporate wealth, privilege, and monopoly, and demanded public ownership or control of warehouses, utilities, and railroads. Immigrants and natives, prohibitionists and suffragettes, farmers, and laborers, in ever-changing coalitions of principle or convenience, attacked social and economic problems. Sometimes they worked through third or minor parties, sometimes they struggled within the primaries of the major parties; but whatever their methods, they fought with righteous zeal for their conceptions of social justice and good government.

In the dynamics of Minnesota politics, party lines have never seemed sacred. Significant numbers of voters show no hesitancy in crossing over, splitting their ticket, supporting "the man rather than the party." In 1956 a majority of Minnesotans voted for the Republican presidential candidate, Dwight D. Eisenhower, while electing a Democratic governor, Orville L. Freeman. In 1960 the reverse was true: a Democratic presidential candidate (John F. Kennedy) and a Republican gubernatorial candidate (Elmer L. Andersen) received Minnesota's votes. Similar situations occurred in earlier decades. In 1904 and 1908 the election results paired a Republican president (Theodore Roosevelt and William Howard Taft) and a Democratic governor (John A. Johnson). In the national elections of the 1940's Democrats Franklin D. Roosevelt and Harry S. Truman won the state's presidential electors, but Republicans Harold E. Stassen, Edward J. Thye, and Luther W. Youngdahl captured the governorship. The

4

independent spirit of the Minnesota voter is a significant political fact of life in the state. It may be traced in part to the third-party tradition and in part to the tradition of nonpartisan elections of local officials as well as state legislators, both of which have increased the fluidity of party alignments.

At the same time there has been no absence of intense partisanship in Minnesota — lively, raucous, bitter party battles have colored the state's history down to the present, when two strong major parties contend for votes — and power — in campaigns less physically violent perhaps than some of the past, but no less verbally vigorous. And the political leaders who have put their mark on the state, and have claimed national attention as well, have been closely associated with party movements. Hubert H. Humphrey, the Democratic candidate for the presidency in 1968, and Eugene J. McCarthy, his chief opponent in that year for the Democratic presidential nomination, are the latest in this line of imaginative and controversial men, which includes Ignatius Donnelly, sometime Republican, Anti-Monopolist, Greenbacker, Populist; Democrat John A. Johnson; Farmer-Laborite Floyd B. Olson; and Republicans Harold E. Stassen and Luther W. Youngdahl. They and the several parties whose fortunes they shared and influenced have contributed richly to the shaping of the present political character of the state.

It is appropriate, then, to begin this brief introduction to politics in Minnesota by tracing certain of the party patterns in the period of its statehood. A comprehensive political history cannot be attempted here. But it is hoped that the sketch that follows, incomplete though it is, will set the scene, so to speak, for the discussion of special characteristics of contemporary Minnesota politics in later chapters. Some of the names and dates and statistics that must be omitted in the narrative will be found in the supplementary materials at the end of this book.

Republican hegemony, 1858–1904

The state of Minnesota was born in an era of high partisan feelings. Even during the territorial period questions concerning the extension of slavery, prohibition of liquor traffic, railroad and land speculation, and voting rights for immigrants divided Democrats from newly created Republicans and sparked impressive displays of fervor and invective.

But the most dramatic demonstration of party hostility came in the state constitutional convention of 1857. With a frontier society's disregard for procedural niceties, it had been called by a special session of the territorial legislature which did not have a right to call it, and upon the signature of a governor who had no right to so act while outside the territorial limits; it was attended by more delegates than were entitled to accreditation; and it permitted participation by some whose certificates were issued in clear violation of the letter and spirit of the election laws. Nearly six weeks were required to organize the convention, and even then the delegates refused to assemble in the same room; they never deliberated as one body and never affixed their signatures to a single document. Minnesota still preserves two basic charters, one drafted and signed by the Democratic wing of the convention, the other by the Republican wing. Both are official. Though they are substantially alike, there are more than three hundred minor differences in punctuation and phraseology.

The first gubernatorial election was likewise the occasion of intense rivalry between the parties. After a bitter campaign, a Democrat, Henry H. Sibley, became the first governor of the state in 1858. But a Republican, Alexander Ramsey, replaced him in 1860, and for most of four decades thereafter the Republican party dominated Minnesota. From 1860 to 1904 only one non-Republican was elected governor; the state legislature remained under Republican control except for the 1891 session; 36 of the state's 50 representatives in Congress during this period were Republicans. Minnesota voters consistently supported Republican presidential candidates by heavy majorities.

Republicanism did not rule unchallenged, however. This was a period of explosive growth in population, from 172,000 in 1860 to 1,751,000 in 1900, and of rapid social and economic change; when the party in power did not respond quickly enough in satisfying new needs and curbing new abuses, one or another of a succession of third parties appeared as the highly vocal champion of reform. The Democrats too, while relatively ineffective at the polls and badly torn by internal dissension, remained critics to be reckoned with. The political winds stirred up by rival parties were felt in Republican councils and influenced to some extent Republican policy. At the state level, as at the national, a number of the specific reforms espoused by protest groups found their way into major party platforms, and finally into law.

In Minnesota agrarian discontent was the focus of third-party movements, as declining prices, discriminatory railroad practices, tight credit, and the currency shortage squeezed the once self-sufficient farmer. Wheat became king in the state, and farmers were ever-increasingly dependent for their livelihood upon the huge corporations that regulated the transportation and sale of their major crop. The platforms of the Anti-Monopolists, the Greenbackers, the Farmers' Alliance, and the Populists from the 1870's through the 1890's crystallized the grievances of the farmer. The railroads were condemned for their discriminatory practices, their unscrupulous collusion with warehouse and elevator interests, their watered stock; Minneapolis wheat combines were accused of ruthless speculation and monopolistic price-fixing. As early as 1873 the Anti-Monopolists and Greenbackers demanded state surveillance of corporations and railroads.

Minnesota third parties did not, however, limit their interests to the welfare of farmers only. In 1872 the Prohibition party called for the immediate enfranchisement of women. In 1879 the Greenbackers advocated a "graduated and equitable" income tax and an outright end to the employment of children under fourteen. In 1888 the Farm and Labor party demanded the Australian ballot, the eight-hour day, employer liability for workmen's injuries, and a sizable number of other reforms.

Implicit in the programs of all these groups was a new concept of government — the idea that the state should take unto itself greater responsibility for economic justice, exercising its latent powers to protect the public interest against private privilege.

One of the most colorful personalities associated with Minnesota third parties was Ignatius Donnelly. A man of wide-ranging literary and social as well as political interests, Donnelly has been called "the universal genius of the prairies." During his eventful career he was elected lieutenant governor and representative to Congress under the Republican banner; he served in the state legislature as an independent; he was spokesman for one third-party movement as editor of the *Anti-Monopolist*; he was an unsuccessful candidate for governor on the Populist ticket in 1892; and at one time or another he held positions of importance with the several agrarian reform groups. His powers of oratory were considerable, and his energy boundless, but another Minnesota liberal, Sidney M. Owen, Farmers' Alliance candidate for governor in 1890 and editor of *Farm, Stock and Home*, was a steadier and perhaps a more influential leader in the state's protest politics.

Although Owen was defeated for governor the protest movement had a taste of victory in 1890, for the Farmers' Alliance and Democrats took advantage of a three-party deadlock to capture both houses of the legislature. But the Republicans regained control in 1892, and not until 1898 did the various protest groups cooperate effectively to elect a governor. In that year, John Lind, supported by Democrats, Populists, and Silver Republicans, was swept into office.

But radical reform was not in the offing. Lind himself was by no means a rabid reformer, and he was powerless to carry even his moderate program against a solid Republican front in the legislature. He served only one term, and Republican governors were elected in 1900 and 1902.

In 1904, however, the Republican dynasty was broken, by the 43-year-old editor of the *St. Peter Herald*, John A. Johnson.

A Democratic interlude, 1904–1910

In a Horatio Alger era Johnson was an embodiment of the rags to success tradition. He was born on a farm near St. Peter, into a Swedish immigrant family less than ten years in their new country. His blacksmith father succumbed to alcoholism, deserted the family, and died later in a poorhouse, leaving Mrs. Johnson to take in washing and her 13-year-old son to begin a career that was finally to put him in the governor's chair for three terms and bring nomination for the presidency within view.

Successful as a journalist (he was elected president of the Minnesota Editorial Association at the age of 32), Johnson was at first unsuccessful in his bid for the state legislature, but in 1898 he was elected to the senate. His vigorous campaigning and political acumen in the legislature caught the attention of the state Democratic leaders, and he became their gubernatorial candidate in 1904.

These were days before the automobile, radio, and television brought candidates ubiquitously to the electorate, but in a month and a half Johnson barnstormed through 74 of Minnesota's then 84 counties to deliver a total of 102 speeches. Republican strength, already sapped by internal feuds, wilted before such a barrage, and Johnson defeated his Republican opponent by 7,000 votes — this while Theodore Roosevelt was carrying the state 216,000 to 55,000 over Alton B. Parker. He was re-elected in 1906 by a 74,000 majority, and his popularity remained strong in 1908.

Johnson was a "reform" governor, who drew on Populist and other progressive support. He was devoted to conservation, to curtailment of railroad abuses, to protecting the public weal against utility privileges; he never hesitated to defend the downtrodden. But he never lost his sense of proportion; he was never a demagogue.

The legislature remained under Republican control during Johnson's tenure in office. But he secured bipartisan backing for a number of significant measures. Codes were enacted regulating insurance companies and timber sales on state lands. Inheritance laws were tightened. Railroads were prohibited from issuing free passes to officeholders, thus ending an abuse long decried by reform groups because it opened the door to "undue influence,"

9

if not to outright peculation, by public officials who rode free but collected travel allowances from the public treasury. Another long-time plank of third-party platforms became law when cities were empowered to own and operate public utilities.

Johnson's achievements were bringing him a national reputation, enhanced by speaking engagements throughout the country. To Democrats who found William Jennings Bryan too radical for comfort, Johnson seemed an attractive alternative. A few Johnson-for-President clubs sprang up around the country in 1908, but Bryan had a long head start, and the Democratic National Convention gave him 888½ votes to Johnson's 46. The Minnesota governor was still very young for a presidential candidate, however, only 47, and his supporters looked forward eagerly to 1912.

Then, in 1909, following abdominal surgery, Johnson died. Ordinarily non-demonstrative Minnesotans "wept in the streets," and some fifty thousand people viewed his body as it lay in state. He had been the "people's governor," as his biographer calls him, and their sense of loss at his death was deep and personal. His death also ended the first sustained Democratic leadership in the state, for during two decades after 1910 (with the exception of one two-year term), Republicans again dominated the governorship.

Republican progressivism and farmer-labor protest, 1910–1930

Minnesota Republicanism during the 1910's and 1920's was strongly tinged with Roosevelt progressivism. Theodore Roosevelt carried the state in 1912 against Woodrow Wilson and William Howard Taft, and he long remained a popular symbol for liberal Republicans and for third-party mavericks, who found themselves much in sympathy with the governmental reforms he advocated: direct primaries, conservation of resources, curbing of trusts and special interests, for example.

During the Republican administrations of these years in Minnesota, legislative beginnings were made in such fields as cooperative marketing, grain grading, workmen's compensation, and aid to veterans in the form of bonus or tuition. A statewide primary law was adopted. Elections to the legislature were put on a nonpartisan basis. The highway system was expanded. A state Industrial Commission was created, as well as a rural credit system empowered to invest state funds in farm mortgages. Especially during the three terms of Theodore Christianson (1925–31), the administrative system of the state was reconstructed.

It was the Nonpartisan League that disturbed Republican calm in this period.

The League had been formed in 1915 by a group of North Dakota farmers under the inspired leadership of A. C. Townley. Its primary purpose was to secure public ownership of certain essential farm services and facilities — terminal elevators, flour mills, packing houses, and so on — so that farmers would not be at the mercy of irresponsible private enterprise. "Nonpartisan" in principle, the League was not conceived as a separate political party but was to work for the candidates of its choice through the primaries and conventions of the established parties.

Likened by one historian to a prairie fire, the League swept swiftly over North Dakota and spread to Minnesota, where its program made sense to Red River Valley and western Minnesota wheat farmers long resentful of middlemen, of the railroads, and of the Minneapolis grain exchange. The spirit of Populism was still very much alive among Minnesota farmers, and it responded quickly to the ingenious tactics of the League organizers. There was nothing subtle about the way Townley and his lieutenants descended on Minnesota in 1917. Specially trained organizers came in caravans of 80 or 90 cars and went to work systematically canvassing rural areas under the direction of small committees of local farmers.

Dedicated adherents multiplied — but so did opponents. And the League was vulnerable to attack in the war years of 1917 and 1918 because of the heavy German cast of its membership and because of the antiwar stand taken by a number of its leaders before the United States entered World War I. The Minnesota Public Safety Commission, directed by Governor Joseph A. A. Burnquist and Judge John F. McGee, was established to scrutinize groups suspected of being disloyal, and the League came under its severe condemnation. "A Nonpartisan League lecturer," said Judge McGee, "is a traitor every time. In other words, no matter what he says or does, a League worker is a traitor."

Townley and one of his aides were arrested, charged with anti-war conduct; injunctions against League meetings were issued in nineteen counties; mob violence erupted here and there. Even so, the embattled Nonpartisan candidate for governor in the Republican primary of 1918, former Congressman Charles A. Lindbergh, although defeated, received 150,000 votes, a remarkable show of strength.

The League had early recognized that in Minnesota farm support would not be enough to win elections: the state's urban vote, much larger than in North Dakota, must also be tapped. Relations were established with labor groups as early as 1917, and in 1920 the League and the Working People's Nonpartisan Political League, made up of union members, supported a joint slate of candidates for state office, which was defeated. In 1922, after an attempt to fuse with the Democrats had failed, League adherents campaigned independently as the Farmer-Labor party; their candidate for governor, Magnus Johnson, came within 14,000 votes of winning and Farmer-Laborites did capture three congressional seats, two in the House and one in the Senate. The following year the Farmer-Labor group won the state's second Senate seat in a special election after the death of the incumbent.

But even this modest success was short-lived. It had been due in part to a sharp decline in farm prices, and with a general economic upswing in the middle twenties, and an accompanying conservative reaction, the new party's fortunes faltered. They were further undermined by the tactics of the American Communist party in the campaign preceding the national election of

1924. The Communist attempts to infiltrate the national third party that was supporting Robert M. LaFollette for president — with which the Minnesota Farmer-Labor group had strong ties — were widely publicized. LaFollette himself denounced the Communists, and the Farmer-Labor gubernatorial candidate, Floyd B. Olson, while failing to take the matter seriously enough to make a strong stand, denied Communist leanings. Public confidence was shaken, however, and the Communist issue contributed to the decisive defeat of state and national reform-party candidates.

Through the rest of the twenties, continued prosperity and the respected leadership of Governor Christianson kept the capitol in St. Paul a Republican stronghold.

The Farmer-Labor party in office, 1931–1939

With the Great Depression, what had been a radical element in the political ideology of the minority — governmental responsibility for the economic and social welfare of all citizens — became an imperative majority demand. The clamor for government action on behalf of the individual — the unemployed, the hungry, the distressed — united at least temporarily farmers and laborers, small-business men, white-collar workers, and intellectuals. As the farm economy collapsed, businesses failed by the score, and industry slowed to snail's pace, Minnesotans, with the rest of the nation, looked for a political deliverer. In Floyd B. Olson they found a man whose temperament and abilities well suited the times — a rebel willing to try the unorthodox, a humanitarian deeply committed to the defense of the underprivileged, a leader of great personal magnetism who inspired devotion and confidence.

Like John A. Johnson, Olson came of Scandinavian immigrant stock. Like his predecessor too, Olson learned at first hand the problems of the "have nots." After a year at the University of Minnesota, he left his home on Minneapolis' north side to knock about the outside world as salesman, miner, and common laborer. His experience vastly broadened, he returned to Minneapolis,

13

put himself through night law school, and embarked on a promising law practice. But his lifelong restlessness pushed him to livelier fields, and he sought and won the post of Hennepin County attorney.

Although he was a crusader against racketeering and city hall corruption, he showed genuine sympathy for petty criminals, whom he considered victims of an unjust social order rather than incorrigibles meriting severe punishment. He also championed organized labor against conservative business.

After his defeat in the 1924 gubernatorial race, Olson restricted his activities to Minneapolis for a time, but he kept his political fences in good repair and slowly began to build a reservoir of personal support — among Democrats and some Republicans as well as the stalwarts of the young Farmer-Labor party. He was ready when his opportunity came in 1930.

The campaign of that year was reminiscent of the crusades of Greenbackers, Progressives, and Nonpartisan Leaguers, as the young county attorney led the Farmer-Laborites to a resounding victory on a platform advocating many of the traditional third-party reforms, as well as immediate relief for the destitute. In winning the governorship, Olson carried 82 of the state's 87 counties. But his party captured only one of the state constitutional offices besides the governorship and only 29 state senatorships and 40 seats in the state house of representatives.

Despite the Farmer-Labor landslide, then, Olson did not enjoy a legislative majority during his first term, and his program had heavy going. But the 1932 election, which returned Olson to office with 50.6 percent of the popular vote against 32.3 percent for the Republicans and 16.4 percent for the Democrats, also gave him substantial backing in the legislature. Important parts of his program were subsequently enacted into law: a mortgage moratorium bill was passed, protecting hard-pressed farmers against foreclosure; a state income tax was adopted; labor injunctions and "yellow dog" contracts were prohibited; a beginning was made in old-age pensions. However, the more extreme planks of the Farmer-Labor platform, such as public ownership of utilities and factories, unemployment and health insurance, outlawing of loan sharks, free distribution of school textbooks, and reduction of interest rates, were rejected.

During his three terms as governor, Olson was forced to weather one crisis after another: the deepening depression; the bloody Minneapolis truckers' strike of 1934; the Farm Holiday Association's march on the state capitol; bitter factional struggles for prestige and patronage within his own party, and embarrassing indiscretions of friends and appointees.

But Olson thrived on controversy. And his powerful personality and striking accomplishments in Minnesota were bringing him national prestige. In Washington, where he frequently represented the state, he was respected as one of the most effective of the nation's liberal governors. There was considerable support in 1936 for a national third-party ticket headed by Olson — support which he did little to encourage, for he was unwilling to hurt Franklin D. Roosevelt's chances in Minnesota.

At 45 Olson seemed promising presidential timber for the future. But, again, tragedy struck a favorite son of Minnesota. Late in the summer of 1936, on the eve of the election campaign in which he had hoped to run for the Senate, Floyd B. Olson died. The affection of the state's people for their fallen leader poured out in emotional torrents — as it had a generation or so earlier for Johnson. Friend and adversary alike joined in uncritical sorrow and praise.

In calmer perspective Olson may be seen as a figure of considerable stature in the protest-party tradition of the state, though by no means without failings, personal and political. A rebel at heart — "I am not a liberal," he once shouted; "I am what I want to be — I am a radical" — he was regarded by conservatives as little better than a card-carrying Communist. Yet his radicalism was perhaps pragmatic rather than theoretical; he saw welfare legislation on behalf of the farmer, the unemployed, and the aged in terms of simple social justice. At any rate, wherever his sympathies tended, his political skill was such that during most of his administration he managed to keep in

15

harness the more radical and the more conservative elements in the Farmer-Labor coalition.

Olson's fellow Farmer-Laborite Elmer Benson, who succeeded to the governorship in 1937, had no such skill. His difficulties were compounded by a resurgence of the Communist issue. Olson had likewise been plagued by Communist activities, but they came to a head during the Benson administration.

Challenges from the far left were not new in Minnesota. As we have seen, they harassed the Farmer-Labor movement of the twenties. Even earlier, various offshoots of European Marxism appeared in Minnesota. Numerically, these parties were never significant, rarely polling more than 1 percent of the entire vote and at no time more than 10,000 for a state or federal office. Yet, since they campaigned vigorously and criticized the major parties relentlessly, they were of importance out of proportion to their size.

At the risk of greatly oversimplifying a complex matter, one might distinguish several major strains of American Marxism. First there were the "direct actionists" or revolutionary syndicalists. With the workers' syndicate or union as their social unit and with strikes, boycotts, and if necessary violence as their means, they aimed to exterminate capitalism and transform society, and to do all this without recourse to existing political methods and institutions. In Minnesota the group showing closest kinship to this tradition of irreconcilable class war was the Industrial Labor or Socialist Labor party (1900), which was affiliated with the national faction led by Daniel DeLeon. (The present-day Industrial Government party, which polled 5,231 votes in the 1966 contest for election to the United States Senate, is often considered to be the ideologically orthodox but nonviolent and anti-Communist successor to the DeLeon tradition.)

Second, political socialism as practiced by several different groups reflected two opposed interpretations of Marxism, the one a moderate revisionism and the other a radical communism. Followers of the former theory insisted that socialism could be achieved through democratic means — by ballots rather than bullets; their aim was public ownership and/or control of basic industry. Candidates of their persuasion customarily used the Socialist or Public Ownership label when running for office. After Lenin founded the Third International in 1919 and welded it into an instrument to direct radical Marxism in its worldwide battles, the more moderate socialists found themselves locked in acrimonious conflict with aggressive and totalitarian communism. Echoes of their internecine warfare were heard as far away as Minnesota's northern Finnish communities, where the so-called "Red" Finns disputed with the other Finnish socialist factions. Rallying around the perennial candidate Norman Thomas, the moderate socialists in Minnesota and elsewhere condemned Leninist-Stalinist terrorism as a gross perversion of Marxist theory; no less critical of Kremlinist communism were the Trotsky followers who appeared on Minnesota's presidential ballot as the Socialist Workers party in 1948.

Although as early as 1920 William Z. Foster, leader of the official American Communist party, the Kremlin-recognized affiliate of the Third International, labeled the Farmer-Labor movement a party of the petty bourgeoisie, corrupt and opportunistic, a betrayer of the proletariat, his followers did not hesitate to attempt to infiltrate the group in 1924. In 1933 and 1934 the Communists exploited farmer-labor grievances and organized marches on the state capitol and mass demonstrations. Then, suddenly, a significant shift occurred in Communist world tactics. The new program of the Soviet Union (1935–36) was to create a grand alliance, a "popular front" of anti-Fascist and pro-democratic elements. In the United States, New Deal groups, the CIO, and many other organizations (including the Minnesota Farmer-Labor party) were to be cultivated and used as fronts for the new strategy. Leftist agitators were to play on Americans' sympathy for the Spanish Loyalists and horror at the growing Nazi menace. Though they were decent, sensitive, and fundamentally honest people, a few of the followers of the midwestern protest tradition fell victim to the Moscow line, which cleverly and callously used catchwords out of their own ideological heritage.

Governor Benson was deaf to critics in his own administration who warned him of the danger of betrayal of midwestern liberalism inherent in Communist tactics. Making little effort to conceal his annoyance, Benson termed such admonitions the irresponsible smears of business interests seeking to cloud the true issues of unemployment and social injustice. At the same time legislative investigations of irregularities in the state Highway, Conservation, and Relief departments were providing additional political capital for critics.

The Farmer-Laborites were badly divided as the 1938 election approached. In a bitter campaign marked by extremes of vituperation, Hjalmar Petersen challenged incumbent Elmer Benson in the Farmer-Labor primary. Claiming to be the legitimate political heir of Olson, Petersen alleged that his opponent had "stolen" the party nomination in 1936 with the help of a "palace guard"; he accused the Benson administration of incompetence and indifference to Communist infiltration. This public washing of Farmer-Labor dirty linen was particularized by reporter Joseph H. Ball in the *St. Paul Dispatch-Pioneer Press,* whence Republicans picked up details to good effect in fall campaigning. Though he survived the primary, Benson's vote-getting appeal had been irreparably damaged.

Farmer-Labor rule, then, was doomed and waiting only for the *coup de grâce.* This came at the hands of Harold E. Stassen, a young Dakota County attorney, who amassed in 1938 the largest majority ever received by a Minnesota governor up to that time.

Republican resurgence, 1939–1955

According to some sources, Stassen had had political and even presidential aspirations as far back as his high school days. After a brilliant career at the University of Minnesota, where he took a law degree, he soon turned to active politics. Convinced of his own mission and persuaded of the haplessness of Republican leadership, he began during the depths of the Depression, in 1934, to make the party over by means of a Young Republican League. This movement attracted professional people, anti-leftist Progressives, young businessmen, reformers, and thousands more who could find political fellowship neither among the intransigent Republicans nor among the scandal-ridden Farmer-Laborites. While making a firm distinction between socialism and his own "enlightened capitalism," as he called it, Stassen was not blind to the usefulness of the milder New Deal proposals, as for example social legislation for the needy, the aged, and the dependent.

His 1938 campaign concentrated on a few essentials. In addition to capitalizing on the Communist issue, he advocated a civil service law to prevent in the future the patronage abuses which had discredited the Farmer-Laborites; new legislation to stabilize management-labor relations and prevent bloody strikes; administrative reorganization to save public money, increase efficiency, and preclude corruption and racketeering.

Farmer-Laborites scoffed at Stassen's claim to kinship with midwestern liberalism and progressivism. Was he not, they asked, the spokesman for United States Steel, meatpackers, and the utilities? The Republican old guard was hardly more enthusiastic about the "Boy Scout," as they termed him; they resented his youth (he was only 31 when elected) and his open cultivation of an "all-Stassen" organization. But he had an excellent press, largely due to the efforts of reporter Joseph Ball, and he drew heavy support from customarily independent or nonpolitical segments of the electorate as well as from a hard core of young Republicans.

As the nation's youngest governor in 1939, Stassen achieved an impressive record. Under his leadership, the Minnesota legislature adopted a civil service system, increased social security benefits, extended the moratorium on mortgages, passed an anti-loan-shark bill. Stassen's reorganization of the state administration, his labor relations record, and his steady internationalism in the midst of pre-Pearl Harbor isolationism earned him widespread respect.

He was not without critics. His administration was accused of granting tax reductions to iron-ore companies, of permitting preferential tax valuations on utility company properties, and of inserting an old-age lien law into the old-age assistance program. Even more violently condemned was the "summer housecleaning" of 1939 which removed an unspecified number (the estimates range from 2,252 to 10,000) of Farmer-Labor appointees or sympathizers from public office just before the new civil service law went into effect.

On the whole, however, Stassen's program was highly regarded by Minnesota voters. A 1939 Gallup poll showed that 81 percent of those queried approved his actions, and only 19 percent disapproved. His large majorities in the 1940 and 1942 elections reaffirmed this popularity.

After 1939 foreign policy and the war loomed large in Minnesota politics. When isolationist Senator Ernest Lundeen died in 1940, Stassen appointed to complete the unexpired term his old friend and press advocate Joseph Ball, a confirmed internationalist like Stassen himself. Few appointments in the state's history caused more of a stir than this one. Although Ball had propelled the virtually unknown Stassen into prominence and had aided immeasurably his first campaign, Republican regulars were bitterly disappointed that Stassen had not rewarded a man of richer governmental experience and unquestioned party loyalty. But Stassen felt strongly that the troubled times required a man with the outlook of Ball. Both Stassen and Ball represented a break with the old midwestern tradition of isolationism which had been so powerfully articulated by Congressmen Charles A. Lindbergh, Harold Knutson, and Ernest Lundeen — all of whom had vigorously opposed United States entry into World War I.

In 1943 Stassen left Minnesota for service with the United States Navy, where his tour of duty as flag officer to Admiral W. F. Halsey enhanced his stature, as did his later participation in the United Nations charter conference in San Francisco.

Stassen had his baptism in presidential politics in 1940, when he was floor manager for the successful nomination campaign of

Wendell L. Willkie at the Republican National Convention. In 1948 he made his own serious bid for the nomination, but tactical miscalculations (contesting Taft delegates in the Ohio presidential preference primary, for example) caused rifts between him and the party regulars, and the convention gave its support to Thomas E. Dewey.

During the next four years as president of the University of Pennsylvania, he attempted to put down new political roots in the nationally influential keystone state, in preparation for the 1952 Republican convention. But this was to be the scene of deep disappointment for Stassen — and, ironically, it was developments in Minnesota that dealt the decisive blow to his hopes.

Stassen had led in the Minnesota Republican presidential primary, and most of the state's convention delegates were officially pledged to him. But a write-in campaign for Dwight D. Eisenhower, launched just a few days before the state primary, had resulted in what came to be called the "Minnesota miracle." With almost none of the advance publicity Stassen had enjoyed, and without the approval and aid of the national Eisenhower organization, the campaign was phenomenally successful: 108,692 voters took the trouble to write in Eisenhower's name on the ballot, while Stassen, whose name was printed thereon, received only some 20,000 more votes, 129,076. The majority of the Minnesota delegates to the convention took this as a popular mandate for the general turned college president, and before the first roll call had been officially closed the delegation switched its vote from Stassen to Eisenhower. Thus ended Stassen's second bid for the nomination.

Although appointed to high posts in the Eisenhower administration, Stassen was unsuccessful in later bids for elective public office in Pennsylvania and in renewed campaigns for the presidential nomination in the 1960's. A resourceful and creative leader, with a keen mind and boundless energy, he perhaps carried within him the flaw of the traditional tragic protagonist; certainly his ill-concealed overriding ambition for power, together with an apparent opportunism and basic errors in political judgment, contributed to his reverses. At any rate he was never able to recapture the place he once held in the popular imagination as the boy wonder of Minnesota.

In 1943 Stassen had been succeeded in the Minnesota governorship by Lieutenant Governor Edward J. Thye, under whom the Stassen tradition was further developed. A major contribution of his administration was the establishment of the first Interracial Commission in the state. He remained in office until 1946, when he was elected to the United States Senate. Luther W. Youngdahl, who had served with distinction as a judge in district court and state supreme court, continued the Republican gubernatorial line.

In his public pronouncements during his three terms as governor, Youngdahl, a devout Swedish Lutheran, proclaimed the moral imperative of Christian participation in politics. Putting into practice his own philosophy that "Christian conscience" must be brought to bear on all phases of public as well as private life, he directed the energies of his administration toward the problems of youth, law enforcement, mental health, and human relations. Significant legislation was accomplished. The youth conservation act of 1947 provided for specialized rehabilitation treatment for juvenile offenders; the anti-slot-machine act of 1947 was designed to curb all major forms of gambling; a comprehensive mental health act was adopted in 1949. By executive decree Negroes were admitted into the National Guard on an integrated basis. From the podium and the pulpit Youngdahl campaigned throughout the state for these and other reforms which gained enthusiastic support from socially conscious members of divergent religious and political faiths; proposals for the granting of the power of arrest to liquor control officers and for a statewide Fair Employment Practices Commission are further examples.

The Republican party during the Youngdahl era was an interesting amalgam of old-guard stalwarts, former Stassenites, newcomers attracted by the governor's reforms, and temporarily Republican independents. When Youngdahl accepted a federal district judgeship in the District of Columbia in July 1951, the *Minneapolis Star* was moved to comment: "With Youngdahl out of the picture, one observer has suggested Republicans can go back to being Republicans and Democrats to voting for Democrats."

This is not to say that Youngdahl enjoyed a five-year political honeymoon. Critics were not lacking who objected to what they considered clothing partisan politics in the garb of moral righteousness; others saw his tireless campaigning on the issues of mental health, youth conservation, and law enforcement as a convenient evasion of less dramatic but pressing governmental problems of administrative reform, tax reform, and so on; still others, especially among conservative, economy-minded legislators, found the costs of his New Dealish social-welfare program alarming. Frustration over stubborn legislative resistance to parts of his program in 1951 may have been a factor in Youngdahl's decision to leave the governorship for the bench.

C. Elmer Anderson, who had served as lieutenant governor under Stassen, Thye, and Youngdahl, succeeded to the governorship and retained the post in the 1952 election. He continued the basic administrative policies and legislative direction set by his predecessors.

Among the veteran Republican officeholders of this era were Mike Holm, Julius A. Schmahl, and Stafford King. Holm held office as secretary of state from 1921 until his death in 1952. Schmahl served as chief clerk of the house in 1902, 1903, and 1905, as secretary of state from 1907 until 1921, and as state treasurer from 1927 until his death in 1957 (1937–39 excepted). After directing the state Department of Soldier Welfare from 1925 to 1931, Stafford King was elected state auditor — a position he occupied continuously until his retirement in 1969. The long tenure of these officials, and, in the 1950's, the election and re-election of men like Republican Val Bjornson, state treasurer, demonstrated the tendency of Minnesota voters to keep in office men whose integrity and judgment they trusted, regardless of what political winds were blowing.

23

POLITICS IN MINNESOTA

Three terms under the Democratic-Farmer-Labor party, 1954—1960

The party which in 1954 brought an end to the sixteen-year Republican control of the governorship bore the label Democratic-Farmer-Labor.

In 1944 political necessity had finally effected a fusion between the two major rivals to Republicanism in the state. For twenty years there had been sporadic attempts to join Democrats and Farmer-Laborites, and since 1932 they had been united in national politics by their common support of Franklin D. Roosevelt. But there were obstacles to final union in state politics.

The Democrats were essentially an urban party. They were strong among the Irish and in the Catholic communities in St. Paul, Duluth, and St. Cloud. Their upper-middle-class leadership had conservative inclinations. To many of the Democrats, Farmer-Laborites smacked of radicalism and were too visionary for effective practical politics.

Farmer-Laborites, for their part, had reservations too. They had a strong following among the Scandinavian farmers of northwestern Minnesota and among the organized and politically conscious workers in mining, manufacturing, and railroading. Some had roots in Progressive Republicanism and felt ideologically closer to Republicans than to Democrats, whom they considered political opportunists overly concerned with federal patronage. Others were reluctant to give up the dream of a new national party unpolluted by compromise with either southern bourbons or Wall Street tycoons.

But overriding the considerations of ideology, economics, and ethnic or religious background was the pressing need to win elections. Unless these two parties could close ranks and agree on a single ticket, the Republican party would be virtually assured of continued domination of the statehouse. Only through fusion of forces, too, could maximum support for Roosevelt in 1944 be achieved; hence national Democratic leaders added their weight to the arguments for unification. Accordingly, after protracted negotiation, a new party was welded in convention early in 1944.

24

At the convention a leading role was taken by the man who was to become the party's top vote-getter and most prominent personality — Hubert H. Humphrey.

Humphrey was 33 years old in 1944. The preceding year he had been defeated in the Minneapolis mayoralty race and had become a political science instructor at Macalester College. After participating at the founding of the new party, he was made state DFL campaign manager for the national Roosevelt-Truman ticket. In 1945 he ran again for mayor, and was elected.

As mayor of Minneapolis (to which office he was re-elected in 1947) Humphrey earned the reputation of an effective administrator. He strengthened the role of mayor vis-à-vis the city council; he cracked down on vice, gambling, and corruption; he used to good effect citizens' volunteer committees to make recommendations on housing, veterans' affairs, fair employment practices, and law enforcement. Then in 1948 he became the first Democratic-Farmer-Labor candidate for the United States Senate.

The DFL had achieved a measure of success in 1944 and 1946, electing three of its candidates to Congress. But in 1947–48 it was rocked by one of the most bitter intraparty battles in state history. It pitted left-wing supporters of Henry A. Wallace for president and Elmer Benson for senator against right-wing supporters of Harry Truman for president and Humphrey for senator. Under Humphrey's leadership, the right-wing forces, which included a large group of his former students, young business and professional men and women, labor leaders, and members of farm cooperatives, finally drove the Wallace-Benson faction from the party. Humphrey went on to rout incumbent Republican Senator Ball in the fall election, receiving nearly 60 percent of the vote; the DFL also picked up a fourth House seat.

Several of Humphrey's lieutenants in the 1947–48 party crisis became prominent DFL leaders: Eugenie Anderson, shortly to be appointed United States ambassador to Denmark; Eugene J. McCarthy, United States representative from the 4th District (St. Paul) for ten years, elected to the United States Senate in 1958; Arthur Naftalin, appointed state commissioner of admin-

25

istration in 1954, elected mayor of Minneapolis for four terms in the 1960's; and Orville L. Freeman.

A young lawyer, Freeman became state DFL chairman after the victory of the right-wing forces. As his party's candidate for governor in 1952, he lost to C. Elmer Anderson by more than 160,000 votes. But 1954 brought a sweeping victory to the DFL and Freeman, who again headed the state ticket. In that year too, the Conservatives lost control of the state house of representatives for the first time since the mid-thirties; the Liberal caucus, which organized the house, included strong DFL supporters and maintained close ties with the party. Freeman was re-elected by substantial majorities in 1956 and 1958.

During his three terms Governor Freeman developed effectively the technique of seeking the counsel of citizen-experts in such complex fields as taxation, government ethics, agriculture, consumer credit, and atomic development. Study committees in two fields — taxation and governmental reorganization — conducted exhaustive surveys on the state's resources and needs. In cooperation with business interests, Freeman initiated a vigorous "Sell Minnesota" campaign to encourage economic growth in the state and attract new business and industry. Although the Conservative-controlled senate acted as a brake in the legislature, certain reforms advocated by the governor were enacted: increased benefits in workmen's compensation, unemployment insurance, and old-age assistance; improvements in salary scales for public employees; establishment of a new Department of Corrections; authorization of reapportionment of state legislative districts; extension of the term of executive officers, including governor, to four years (effective with the election of 1962); a good start in revising the election, juvenile, highway, education, and probate codes.

Republican criticism of the Freeman administration centered largely on charges of unnecessary spending; critics also accused DFL officials of being overly friendly toward allegedly lawless elements in labor unions and of mismanagement in the letting of government contracts.

Despite the DFL's solid successes at the polls in 1954, 1956, and 1958, certain internal strains became evident — some growing out of personality conflicts, some having to do with policy differences. In the presidential primary of 1956 an inner party conflict was on public view. Freeman, Humphrey, and most of the state officials stumped vigorously on behalf of Adlai Stevenson. But a number of other party leaders — including influential state Representatives Peter S. Popovich and Donald D. Wozniak of St. Paul — supported Estes Kefauver and made pointed references to "bossism" in connection with the Humphrey-Freeman attempt to marshal the state's Democrats solidly behind Stevenson. When the primary ballots were counted, it was Kefauver and not Stevenson who won the majority of district delegates to the Democratic National Convention. The DFL higher echelon smarted under the double slap from the traditionally independent electorate and from the rebellious element in its own ranks. The conflict left its mark on party unity.

There were also challenges — unsuccessful in the 1950's — to the party's systematic use of pre-primary endorsements. DFL leaders came to support these endorsements strongly, believing them to be largely responsible for the party's success in maintaining its coalition of Farmer-Laborites, old-line Democrats, New Deal city intellectuals, and unionized workers, since pre-primary endorsements meant that all the party's energies could be focused on behalf of one candidate. On the other hand, certain old-time Farmer-Laborites opposed them as an undemocratic, palace-guard device to control the party. In 1954 Paul A. Rasmussen challenged convention-endorsed Orville Freeman in the gubernatorial primary, and in 1958 Hjalmar Petersen ran against convention-endorsed Eugene McCarthy for the senatorial nomination.

A Republican in the governor's chair, 1960–1963

In 1960 the Republicans recaptured the governorship. Their candidate, Elmer L. Andersen, a warmly humane, highly successful St. Paul businessman, had served in the state senate for ten years as a member of the Conservative caucus where he became well known for his liberal leanings. As a senator, he had shown strong interest in education, welfare, metropolitan planning, fair employment practices legislation, programs for Indians, nursing scholarships, mental health clinics, and economic development. In the campaign he attacked Freeman's handling of a strike at the Wilson Company in Albert Lea and charged the DFL administration with failing to hold taxes down and to provide programs that would improve the economically depressed conditions in Minnesota's iron range communities.

It was a close election. Out of a total of more than 1.5 million votes Democrat John F. Kennedy carried Minnesota in the presidential race by 22,000 while Republican Elmer Andersen's margin over Democrat-Farmer-Laborite Orville Freeman for the governorship was 23,800. Continuing to cross party lines, Minnesotans voted for a DFL senator, Hubert Humphrey, a DFL lieutenant governor, Karl F. Rolvaag, a DFL secretary of state, Joseph Donovan, a DFL attorney general, Walter F. Mondale, a DFL railroad and warehouse commissioner, Hjalmar Petersen, a Republican state treasurer, Val Bjornson, and a Republican state auditor, Stafford King. Kennedy later appointed Freeman his secretary of agriculture.

According to the *Minneapolis Tribune*'s "Minnesota Poll," most of Andersen's support came from the smaller cities of the state (50 percent to 44 percent for Freeman), from Protestants (60 percent to 36 percent), from independents (55 percent to 43 percent), and from those age 40 and over (53 percent to 43 percent). As in the past GOP strength was particularly concentrated in the 1st, 2nd, 3rd, and 6th Congressional districts — which are primarily rural in character. Freeman drew most of his support from residents of the Twin Cities (51 percent to 44 percent), from Catholics (65 percent to 28 percent), and from members of organized labor (74 percent to 23 percent). (See Figure 1.)

The 1961 legislature (the house was controlled by the Liberals, the senate by the Conservatives) enacted a fair housing

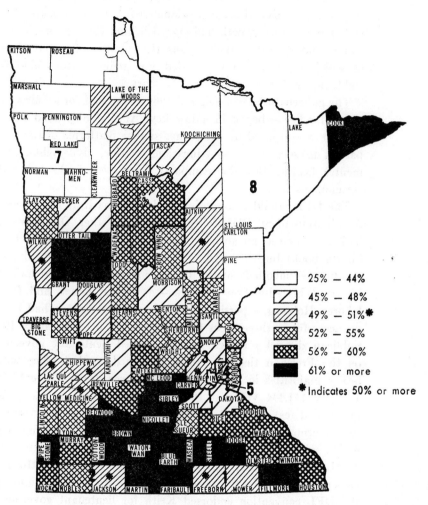

Figure 1. Percentage of Total Vote Received by the
Republican Gubernatorial Candidate in 1960

law and an income-tax-withholding law, revised the state criminal code, authorized additional state parks, and in a special session finally passed a congressional redistricting measure. The state's population growth had lagged behind that of some other states, and after the 1960 census the number of congressmen to which Minnesota was entitled was reduced from nine to eight; thus redistricting became necessary.

The gubernatorial campaign of 1962 — the first for a four-year term of office — began in a low key. At first only mild voter interest was aroused by the rather similar platforms of the two parties in such areas as education, welfare, civil rights, and mental health. But the campaign soon became heated and acrimonious.

The DFL candidate opposing Andersen was Karl F. Rolvaag. An alumnus of St. Olaf College, where his father, Ole Rölvaag, had won fame as an author (*Giants in the Earth* was his best known book) but acquired little money, Karl Rolvaag like so many other members of the Depression generation had had to interrupt his education to work — as logger, miner, and farm laborer. Rolvaag, a persistent and determined fighter, had been unsuccessful in three races for Congress (in predominantly Republican districts) before he was elected lieutenant governor on the Freeman ticket in 1954. Returned to that office with heavy majorities in 1956 and 1958, he was again re-elected in 1960 by 151,444 votes at the same time Freeman was going down to defeat. In 1962 Rolvaag won his party's endorsement for governor only after overcoming opposition from some segments within the DFL, primarily from younger leaders like A. M. (Sandy) Keith who would have preferred that Attorney General Mondale be the party's candidate. In a move for unity the DFL convention endorsed Keith for lieutenant governor.

Two issues came to overshadow all others in the campaign between Andersen and Rolvaag, which reached a stormy climax just before the election: the problem of taconite taxes and the alleged irregularities in the construction of Interstate Highway 35W.

In order to attract increased investments to the iron range, which would lead to greater employment opportunities, Governor Andersen favored a special constitutional amendment guaranteeing that taconite mining companies would not be subjected to heavier taxes than other types of industry. Rolvaag supported equitable taxing of these companies but through the medium of statute rather than constitutional amendment. Eventually the proponents of the constitutional amendment won their case — the 1963 legislature approved it and it was ratified overwhelmingly by the electorate in 1964. This may be regarded as a major personal achievement for Andersen, who worked tirelessly for the amendment, but the influence of this issue on the 1962 election is difficult to assess.

On the other hand the Highway 35 controversy may well have been the decisive factor in the closing days of the campaign. The "Minnesota Poll" indicated that among eligible voters expressing a preference Andersen led Rolvaag by only a few percentage points during the month before the election (in the survey taken the last weekend of October it was Andersen 50 percent, Rolvaag 47 percent), with a substantial number still undecided. Events occurring in the final week obviously could contribute heavily to the way the undecideds voted.

The controversy began in late October with charges made by a highway construction worker (brother of a Rolvaag campaign aide) that there were deviations from federal standards in the construction of Highway 35. Rolvaag claimed that the Andersen administration had exerted pressure to speed up the highway construction schedule so that a special ribbon-cutting ceremony might focus attention on the governor just before the election. Andersen emphatically denied the charges. Whatever the merits of the case (an investigation by the federal Bureau of Roads completed after the election verified some defects but of a relatively minor nature), the flurry of charges and countercharges captured prime headline — and presumably voter — attention.

Senator Humphrey and Congressman John Blatnik of the

31

8th District, chairman of the congressional subcommittee on highway investigations, made effective use of the issue in campaigning for Rolvaag, especially in the 6th and 8th districts. When the votes came in it was clear that support for Andersen in these districts particularly had slipped significantly below his 1960 total; in this the Highway 35 controversy was undoubtedly a critical factor. (See Figure 2.)

The election itself was not to be finally decided for 133 days. At first Rolvaag led by 58 votes out of a total of more than one and a quarter million. But the lead changed frequently as newly corrected returns came in. After almost three weeks the State Canvassing Board, on the basis of the revised returns, declared Andersen the winner by 142 votes. Representatives of Rolvaag petitioned a state district court to order a complete recount. The petition was granted and the nation's first gubernatorial recount was set in motion. Some 800,000 ballots were involved (the tallies from precincts using voting machines had already been rechecked). In the absence of historical and legal precedents, cooperative and innovative action had to be initiated immediately to assure an expeditious and responsible procedure in which the public would have confidence. Helpfully, the state supreme court appointed a panel of three district judges to decide on rules and to make a final adjudication. One hundred three-member inspection teams were set up, each composed of representatives of the candidates and one neutral. Nearly 100,000 ballots were challenged as defective in some way; but special screening panels representing the two candidates reduced the number to a more manageable 1,300. These were brought before the panel of district judges.

The judges construed the applicable statutes liberally and accepted all ballots where the intent of the voters could with assurance be discerned; only those flagrantly invalid were thrown out. When all the categories of ballots had been disposed of, it was found that Rolvaag had 91 more votes than Andersen — a winning margin of .007 percent of the 1,267,507 votes cast. Rolvaag had been provided with an office in the basement of the

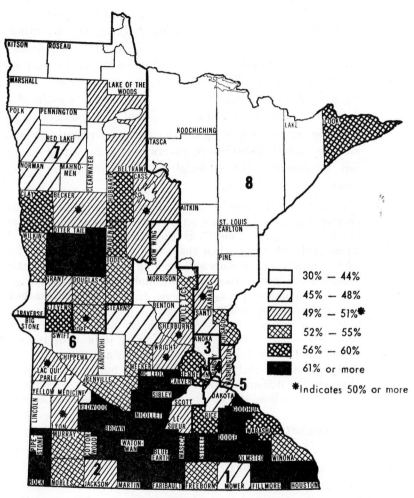

Figure 2. Percentage of Total Vote Received by the Republican
Gubernatorial Candidate in 1962

state capitol while awaiting the outcome of the recount. Finally, on Monday, March 25, 1963, he was sworn in as governor.

Minnesotans can take pride in the entire recount episode. Although instances of looseness and error in the administration of the laws regarding the receiving, tallying, and reporting of votes were uncovered, there was no substantial evidence of intentional wrongdoing or vote stealing in any of the over 2,000 precincts canvassed. More than that, the state's political maturity proved equal to the severe test of four tense months of uncertainty. Despite a tradition of spirited and competitive politics, the public and the partisans remained remarkably calm, and the normal operations of government were carried on without interruption. An editorial in the *Minneapolis Tribune* summed up the situation:

In a recent tongue-in-cheek editorial, the Atlanta Journal commented on the disposition of both Rolvaag and Andersen "to let the courts decide." It then harked back to Georgia's Arnall-Talmadge row when that state had two governors for a while, amid lots of shoving and pushing and with "two adjutants general bossing the troops around, and with everybody signing checks." "Minnesota may be all right," the editorial concluded, "but it must be an awfully dull place."

Perhaps the readiness with which we resort to the judicial processes and our willingness to abide by judicial decisions are characteristics bred in Minnesota — in contrast, say, to some southern states. But "awfully dull" or not, we have passed through the difficult trial of the recount with a becoming respect for the law, the courts and — we hope — each other.

The DFL divided against itself, 1963–1966

When Rolvaag took office the 1963 state legislature — with both houses controlled by Conservatives — had already been in session for almost three months. It was acting on recommendations for appropriations, taxes, and appointments made by Andersen, and the new governor found he could do little to influence the course of legislative action.

In addition to approving the taconite amendment, the legislature created a state-supported junior college system and established a new state college in southwestern Minnesota; approved a system of daytime activity centers for the state's mentally retarded; and adopted a program for long-range development of natural resources in the state.

Two years later Rolvaag and the legislature — still Conservative controlled — came into head-on confrontation. The legislature largely ignored Rolvaag's proposals. The governor in turn vetoed twelve bills, including a reapportionment of state legislative districts which Rolvaag regarded as unconstitutional and inequitable. (Redistricting, which had been ordered by a federal court in 1964, was finally accomplished by a special legislative session in 1966.)

At the same time Rolvaag was having increasing problems with his own DFL party. Party leaders had been unenthusiastic about getting involved in a recount following the 1962 election — some frankly questioned whether the enormous expense would be justified even if their candidate were adjudged the winner; they preferred to look ahead to 1966 when one of the party's vigorous young men would make a strong candidate. The necessary money to pay for the recount was eventually raised and the party hierarchy publicly rejoiced at the result, but Rolvaag had been deeply wounded, as he showed in his staff appointments after taking office. He selected men who had stood loyally by him during the dreary weeks of the recount. Some of them had been active in politics before, but none had held office in the DFL's top echelon. Communication between the governor's office and the party leadership was erratic and relations became severely strained. Further, Rolvaag was not able to project a dynamic public personality and his standing in polls assessing his popularity steadily declined. This did not augur well for the party ticket in 1966, and dissatisfaction with the governor increased in the ranks of party leaders as each new poll was published. An open break with the governor came in the summer of 1965.

It must be acknowledged that the problems that tore the party apart in 1966 were not all of Rolvaag's making. There

35

were the basic differences within the party that went back to its founding days. Certain segments of the labor movement, rural interests, and older party professionals, for example, had never fully reconciled themselves to the new political style and program-oriented approach of the group centering around Humphrey, Freeman, McCarthy, and younger leaders like Walter Mondale (appointed to fill out Humphrey's Senate term when the latter was elected vice-president in 1964), Donald M. Fraser (who defeated veteran Congressman Walter Judd in the 5th Congressional District in 1962), and Sandy Keith, the lieutenant governor of Minnesota. Then, too, as is so often true in American politics, a party's prolonged tenure in power tends to accentuate internal stresses. The DFL had made an impressive electoral record in its short 20-year history and — except for Andersen's one term — it had had control of the governorship since 1955. But after 1962 many of the party's most experienced and competent workers were drafted to staff positions in the national administrations of Kennedy and Johnson; their loss to the state and local party organizations probably intensified the stresses that normally develop within a party long in office.

In July 1965 a DFL conference convened at Sugar Hills, a resort near Grand Rapids, for the purpose of examining internal organizational problems and preparing for an effective legislative election campaign. Rolvaag was invited but did not attend. Toward the end of the meeting, highly critical comments about the governor were made by powerful county and district leaders. Speaker after speaker cited Rolvaag's failure to work with the party, his unfavorable public image, his lackluster legislative and administrative record. Most expressed strong doubts about his chances for re-election. It was agreed that an attempt would be made to persuade him not to run again.

The press had been barred from the Sugar Hills meeting, but details soon appeared in the newspapers. Rolvaag was furious. He felt that he had been betrayed by his party, and he launched a public fight for control of the 1966 convention which would endorse a nominee.

It soon became clear that he would be opposed for the nomination by 35-year-old Lieutenant Governor Keith, an attractive, intelligent, urbane, and successful attorney with good professional and political credentials. In 1958, after Amherst, Yale Law School, and the Marine Corps, Sandy Keith had been sent to the Minnesota senate by his Rochester constituents; in 1962 he was elected lieutenant governor by a comfortable margin. Sporting the Kennedy look and style, Keith was highly popular on college campuses and readily identified with the younger members of the party who were growing impatient with the leadership of the "class of 1948." Keith was convinced that the DFL had to renew itself from within if it was to keep the governorship — Rolvaag had to go for the good of the DFL program. Keith had the support of a number of those who had been at Sugar Hills.

The Rolvaag and Keith forces fought bitterly in precinct and township caucuses and county and district conventions for delegates to the state convention. An estimated 50,000 DFLers debated in their local meetings the wisdom of dumping an incumbent governor — something that no one could remember a political party ever daring to do. The DFL did do just that at its state convention in June 1966 when it endorsed Keith, but not until after twenty soul-searing ballots.

A surge of public sympathy for Rolvaag encouraged him to challenge Keith in the primary. For two months the party's internal dispute was thoroughly aired before the electorate. When the primary returns came in the governor had scored an impressive personal triumph over his own party organization; in the "twenty-first ballot" — the title of a fascinating book about this campaign — he defeated Keith by a margin of better than two to one. For the first time in DFL history a pre-primary endorsement for governor was not sustained by the party's voters.

Meanwhile the state GOP had avoided a similar intraparty debacle. There were four major contenders for the Republican gubernatorial nomination and seventeen ballots were required in the GOP state convention before one of these was endorsed. But immediately thereafter the unsuccessful candidates gave their support to the nominee, Harold LeVander from South St. Paul, a one-time law partner of Harold Stassen.

The fall election campaign saw a remarkably united GOP conduct a vigorous and astute attack on the still gravely divided DFL. LeVander and other Republican campaigners freely used the ammunition against Rolvaag stockpiled by Keith in his primary speeches. Rolvaag's sympathy vote eroded rapidly under Republican charges of administrative incompetence.

Two issues told heavily against Rolvaag and the DFL. One was the so-called American Allied Insurance Company scandal. This company had been declared insolvent in 1965 and the DFL state insurance commissioner, Cyrus Magnusson, among others had been indicted for fraud in connection with the company's activities (he was later acquitted). Keith had been affiliated with a subsidiary company but had severed connections before American Allied got into legal difficulties; nevertheless his association with the subsidiary had been used against him in his campaign for the gubernatorial nomination. The shadow of the scandal also fell on Rolvaag, who was accused of not acting promptly against the company when informed of its dubious financial activities. Republicans used the scandal to discredit the DFL generally.

A second damaging issue concerned a budget cut in aids to local school districts which had been ordered in 1963 by Governor Rolvaag on the grounds that the state faced a serious deficiency in its income tax funds. This action, highly unpopular among school officials and their powerful legislative lobby, had been taken despite assurance from the Republican tax commissioner, Rolland Hatfield, a holdover appointment from the Andersen administration, that sufficient resources would be available. As it happened the Hatfield estimates (aided by the 1964 federal tax cut and by economic growth in the state) proved more accurate than those of the governor's staff. Neither Rolvaag's miscalculation nor his acrimonious public debate with

Hatfield enhanced his stature as governor, and the Republicans were quick to capitalize on this issue.

Rolvaag on the other hand pointed with pride to his administration's record of accomplishments. He stressed that employment was up, that the financial health of the state was excellent, that significant progress had been made in state programs related to health, education, and welfare. A spirited Rolvaag whistlestopped across the state, and Vice-President Humphrey and Senators McCarthy and Mondale joined him in the closing days of the campaign and urged the party faithful and independents to support the ticket.

But it was a Republican year. The GOP swept its candidates into all state constitutional offices but one, and gained a seat in the state's congressional delegation. (See Figure 3.)

Republican return to power in 1967

Unlike the Republican parties of other midwestern states, Minnesota's GOP had not suffered heavy losses in the wake of Barry Goldwater's defeat for the presidency in 1964. This was largely due to the political skill and good sense of state Republican chairman Robert Forsythe and his associates.

The Republican leaders had to survive a strong challenge from the party's right wing at the 1964 state convention. The Goldwater drive had begun in Minnesota in the fall of 1963, when residents of heavily conservative rural and small-town-dominated counties joined hands with conservative suburbanites and urban dwellers to support the man they regarded as a "true conservative." As the Goldwater forces began to gain momentum Forsythe and other Republican leaders — most of them politically moderate — agreed on a tactic to prevent a head-on confrontation of the two wings of the party: they would work for the favorite-son candidacy of Dr. Walter Judd, the widely known former congressman. As the state convention opened the delegates were closely divided between supporters of Goldwater and supporters of more moderate presidential candidates, including Judd. But with political finesse Forsythe and the non-Gold-

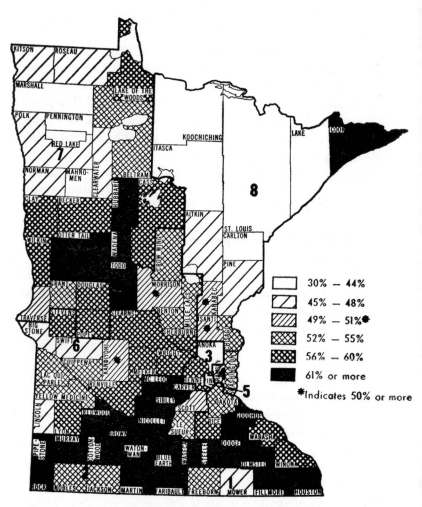

Figure 3. Percentage of Total Vote Received by the Republican
Gubernatorial Candidate in 1966

waterites got control of the convention and elected their slate of at-large delegates to the Republican National Convention. The moderate wing of the party therefore remained in control of the state organization.

At the Republican National Convention former Governor Elmer Andersen supported the moderate position of Nelson A. Rockefeller, with its emphasis on civil rights, on condemnation of both right-wing and left-wing extremism, on the necessity for civilian control of nuclear weapons. Andersen put himself strongly in opposition to the ideological views of Goldwater in a statement he made during the debate over the platform: "The paramount issue of our time, therefore, is how we can best exercise control and who in our country shall decide on our use of nuclear weapons. . . . Putting this type of control in the hands of a field commander [as the platform proposed] . . . is taking control out of the hands of the people through their elected president. It is, in effect, condoning nuclear roulette." This courageous stand was to have repercussions in Minnesota politics, for it made Andersen unacceptable to conservative elements of his party as a candidate for office in the state.

Following the national convention most of the Republican leaders in Minnesota, although not enthusiastic about the Goldwater candidacy, agreed in the interests of party harmony to support the national nominee and work for his election. They were careful, however, to avoid the extremism that might have alienated more moderate Minnesotans and for the most part Republican congressional and legislative candidates did not tie themselves closely to the Goldwater cause.

As a result, while Minnesotans gave their presidential votes to Lyndon Johnson, they also re-elected all incumbent Republican congressmen and returned the Conservative majority to the state house of representatives. The state GOP thus emerged from the 1964 election in a relatively strong position and was able to build for the 1966 state campaign. The unity it showed then, along with the DFL's self-immolation, was undoubtedly an important factor in the Republican victory at the polls in 1966.

When Governor LeVander delivered his first inaugural message on January 4, 1967, he endeavored to set the tone for a "decade of decision . . . an era of resolve unsurpassed in Minnesota history." He called for a new generation of "problem-solvers," of men and women who would seek to understand people, who could motivate the unmotivated, who could create true harmony between the races, who would help senior citizens to a more meaningful life, who would initiate programs that could "set the pace for meeting our present and future problems." The governor urged a system of federal-state tax sharing which would permit the state to assume greater responsibilities for metropolitan growth, for tax relief to the elderly, for economic emancipation of the Indian, for general economic development and tourism, for police training and crime control, for expanded vocational training, for traffic safety and uniform vehicle codes. He requested establishment of a state department of human relations and inclusion of privately financed housing under the state fair housing law, adoption of annual legislative sessions, a state scholarship program, increased state spending for elementary, secondary, higher, and medical education, and strengthening of statewide coordinated planning for the development of higher education programs and facilities.

The 1967 state legislature will be best remembered for some very substantial accomplishments in the areas of education, metropolitan affairs, and taxation. Spending for education reached $717 million, an increase of 31 percent over the preceding biennium. A major expansion in development of state junior colleges was authorized, as were significant improvements in the four-year state colleges.

With respect to metropolitan and urban concerns, the legislature established a metropolitan council of fifteen members, appointed by the governor, for the purpose of coordinating the planning and development of the seven-county metropolitan area (Anoka, Carver, Dakota, Hennepin, Ramsey, Scott, and Washington counties). Also authorized by the legislature was a Department of Human Rights (consolidating a number of existing separate agencies), a Peace Officer Training Board, an Office of Local and Urban Affairs, a Capitol Area Architectural and Planning Commission, an appointive Public Service Commission (in place of the elected Railroad and Warehouse Commission), and a Minnesota Pollution Control Agency.

Enacted over Governor LeVander's veto was the tax reform and relief act of 1967, a far-reaching law and the session's most controversial measure, aimed, according to its supporters, at assuring Minnesota's economic growth and lightening the burden of the state's excessively high local property taxes. The governor had made an explicit campaign promise that he would not sign any sales tax bill that did not provide for a popular referendum, and he determinedly held to his position throughout the session. Conservative leaders in the house and senate were equally determined to pass a 3 percent sales tax even if it meant overriding the Republican governor's veto — which the legislature finally did in a special session.

During the 1969 legislative session, LeVander focused much of his effort on getting approval of a major reorganization of the executive branch of the state government. The legislature did approve a new Department of Public Safety to bring together related services previously scattered in other departments (services connected with criminal apprehension, civil defense, and motor vehicles among others) and significantly increased the power of the governor by giving him authority to shift from one department to another duties, employees, and funds. But the legislature turned down or modified other parts of the governor's reorganization plan.

The 1969 legislature also strengthened the state's human rights act, passed a highly controversial bill allowing publicly financed school bus service to be extended to private and parochial students; approved for submission to the voters constitutional amendments lowering the minimum voting age to 19 and giving the legislature authority to remove certain property from tax-exempt rolls; extended the authority and control of the State Pollution Control Agency; appropriated funds for park

43

and wildlife programs; and increased funds for and broadened the coverage of welfare programs.

Although LeVander did not get from the legislature all he asked for, he did get action on most of his major proposals. Whether this will improve his stature among Minnesota voters remains to be seen. Even his severest critics grant that the governor is a man of high principles, unquestioned personal integrity, and sincere devotion to public duty as well as a tireless salesman of his program. But he has come under heavy criticism, especially for some of his fiscal policies and proposals. During his first two years in office, his popularity (as indicated by the "Minnesota Poll" surveys) declined rather sharply. Whether because of a style of speech more attuned to rural than urban audiences, or insufficient staff assistance, or excessive delegation of certain policy functions to administrative subordinates not overly sensitive to political realities — whatever the reason, Governor LeVander had apparently not been able to communicate to the public an image of effective leadership.

Minnesota's presidential candidates, 1968

In 1968 Minnesota found itself in the unusual position of supplying two major contenders for the presidential nomination of one of the nation's two great parties.

When President Johnson selected Senator Hubert Humphrey to be his running mate in 1964 "as simply the best man in America for the job," many Minnesotans including most DFLers thoroughly rejoiced in the prospect of having the state's favorite son so highly honored. Still, some questioned why Humphrey would wish to leave his influential position of Senate assistant majority leader to serve under the strong-willed and overpowering Lyndon Johnson — in an office that John Adams plaintively characterized as "the most insignificant office that ever the invention of man contrived or his imagination conceived." There were, of course, a number of reasons that have been cited by observers: a sense of public duty, the possibility that the office could be strengthened by an energetic and resourceful incumbent, and the opportunity of being next in line for the presidency — a man with presidential aspirations could hardly fail to be aware that since 1900 alone four vice-presidents — a proportion of one out of three — have succeeded to the highest office in the land.

Whatever Humphrey's precise motivations, it could not have been an easy decision for him to become "number two" — to stand in another man's shadow. His prodigious stamina and will to succeed had already earned him an impressive share of national attention and fame. He had been a co-founder of the DFL party and of the Americans for Democratic Action; at the 1948 Democratic National Convention he had supported a strong civil rights plank, challenging his fellow delegates to recognize that "the time has arrived in America for the Democratic party to get out of the shadows of states' rights and to walk forthrightly into the bright sunshine of human rights"; at the 1956 convention he lost out to Senator Estes Kefauver when he sought the vice-presidential nomination on the Stevenson ticket; four years later, in his first bid for the presidency, he trailed Senator John Kennedy in the Wisconsin and West Virginia primaries; and then in 1961 when Lyndon Johnson left the Senate to become vice-president, Humphrey moved up to become assistant majority leader, or party whip.

It was in the United States Senate that Humphrey achieved his most conspicuous accomplishments. First elected in 1948, Humphrey had to learn that freshmen senators must customarily temper their oratory and eagerness somewhat. But after his re-election in 1954, he rapidly emerged from his apprenticeship to take a place on the Senate's inner council as a powerful though controversial member. His wide-ranging legislative activities and interests extended from foreign policy and social welfare to agriculture and government reform. His committee appointments (including Appropriations, Agriculture, Labor, Public Welfare, Foreign Relations committees; subcommittee chairman on Near Eastern and African affairs) suggest the respect in which his peers held him. His participation in the Eleventh

General Assembly of the United Nations and in UNESCO, along with frequent trips to Europe, the Near East, and the Soviet Union, made him one of the most internationally minded men in Washington. As one of the leading liberals in the upper house, he sponsored and supported legislation on urban renewal, disarmament, arms control, civil rights, welfare, and education. Among his major legislative triumphs was the 1963 Senate ratification of the Limited Nuclear Test Ban Treaty and his imaginative and determined floor leadership of the Civil Rights Act of 1964.

To his well-wishers Humphrey as senator was one of the most effective spokesmen for the New Deal heritage, for minorities, and for social justice. Critics to the left of his own position charged him with inconsistency, if not outright failure of nerve, because of the stand he took when he gave strong support to the Communist Control Act of 1954; the civil-rights defender Humphrey seemed to them in danger of capitulating to the presidential aspirant Humphrey who made friends and alliances among southern colleagues. Right-of-center observers, on the other hand, were alarmed by his early civil-rights stand and feared that his prolabor sympathies would lead him to work hand in glove with Walter Reuther and other labor potentates who sought to turn the Democratic party into a labor party. Still others saw in Humphrey nothing but a glib opportunist with strong demagogic inclinations.

As nominee and then vice-president, Humphrey shared with Lyndon Johnson the landslide victory of 1964 and a heavy workload afterward. In addition to serving on the National Security Council and on special presidential missions to foreign nations, Humphrey acted as chairman of the National Aeronautics and Space Council, the Peace Corps Advisory Council, and the Cabinet Task Force on Youth Opportunity. With typical zeal he became an advocate of the administration's legislative and foreign policy programs before thousands of audiences throughout the nation. As Johnson's popularity declined and the increasingly unsatisfactory progress in Vietnam became more apparent, the vice-president's liberal critics wondered aloud whether Humphrey was not in danger of surrendering his personal integrity by becoming an apologist for a foreign policy that was variously judged morally bankrupt, economically disastrous, or plainly ineffective. Attacks on Humphrey became more vociferous and shrill and the estrangement of college students, black activists, and the ideological left more pointed. To the practitioners of the "new politics" of 1968, Hubert Humphrey had become anathema. Their hero was Humphrey's colleague from Minnesota, Senator Eugene J. McCarthy.

When McCarthy stepped up to the microphone in the Senate caucus room in Washington on November 30, 1967, and announced in thoughtful accents his determination to take the issue of the Vietnam war to the American people, he embarked on a crusade that was to shake the presidency of the United States. Assessing the impact of the McCarthy phenomenon at the time of the 1968 Democratic National Convention, Tom Wicker, chief of the *New York Times* Washington Bureau, concluded that "neither the Democratic party nor American politics is likely to be quite the same again." Nor for that matter, he might have added, would Minnesota's DFL.

McCarthy had taught economics and education at St. John's University and sociology at the College of St. Thomas before his election in 1948 as United States representative from the 4th District. He became known for his leadership among liberal Democrats in the House and for his reflective essays and speeches on political philosophy. In the Senate, following his election in 1958, he sponsored and supported legislation designed to improve the social security program and the unemployment insurance system, to reform the tax structure, to reduce farm surpluses, to limit arms sales by the Defense Department, and to guarantee civil rights to all Americans.

There can be little doubt that McCarthy's struggle against President Johnson was a most unorthodox campaign by a most unorthodox politician. In his quiet, professorial, often witty, and almost always low-key style, McCarthy assailed the moral,

47

military, and foreign policy objectives of the Vietnam war before relatively small audiences on college campuses throughout the country. His bid for the presidential nomination began formally in the wintery hills of New Hampshire. Initially a McCarthy victory over President Johnson and the regular Democratic party slate in the nation's first presidential primary for delegates to the 1968 convention was viewed as most unlikely by most of the professionals. While the leadership of the regulars was admittedly uninspiring and politically inept, all the advantages — power, prestige, patronage — seemed to rest with those who supported the incumbent president. Still, the senator from Minnesota was determined to challenge the establishment. His loyal followers streamed into the state. Leaving campuses and jobs, college students, young professors, movie idols, antiwar activists, and others who believed in the cause came by the hundreds to canvass voters, distribute literature, persuade the doubters. When it was all over, the nation was stunned to learn that McCarthy had won 42.2 percent of the vote and 20 of the 24 convention delegates to which New Hampshire was entitled.

Major political reverberations were quick in coming. Three days after McCarthy's success Senator Robert Kennedy of New York formally announced his entry into the presidential sweepstakes. One of the most dramatic developments of the eventful year of 1968 of course occurred on March 31 when President Johnson announced his intention not to seek another term and to order a partial bombing halt in connection with new moves for peace in Vietnam. How much personal or political credit Senator McCarthy can take for these decisions historians will debate for years to come. Of more immediate consequence was the impact of these events on a number of important political primaries still to be conducted.

McCarthy went on to win a big vote in the Wisconsin primary (56.2 percent), lost narrowly to Senator Kennedy in Indiana, administered the Kennedy family its first major electoral setback in the Oregon primary on May 28, but finally trailed Kennedy again in California.

Following the tragic assassination of Senator Kennedy on June 6 it became quite clear that despite late entries by Governor Lester Maddox of Georgia on the political right and by Senator George S. McGovern of South Dakota on the left, the Democratic party's choice for its 1968 national standard-bearer lay between two Minnesotans — Senator McCarthy and Vice-President Humphrey.

Humphrey officially entered the 1968 presidential race on April 29 and immediately fell heir to most of Johnson's organizational support. Formal backing came quickly from George Meany of the AFL-CIO, from former congressional colleagues, and from party regulars across the nation. His was to be the "politics of joy," a time of "great confidence" and "public happiness" — a reaffirmation of the Kennedy-Johnson and Johnson-Humphrey policies at home and abroad. Avoiding immediate clashes with Senators McCarthy and Robert Kennedy, the vice-president took his case directly to those delegations which had been named in states that did not conduct presidential primaries.

In Minnesota, meanwhile, where the DFL was still reeling from the electoral blows of 1966, the party was once again pulled apart at the seams, this time over the issue of Vietnam. Precinct caucuses held in March gave evidence that McCarthy's position was highly popular throughout many of the urban areas of the state. Minnesota's Concerned Democrats, an anti-war and pro-McCarthy group, scored considerable successes in wresting control from regular Johnson-Humphrey forces in the 3rd, 4th, and 5th Congressional districts and in such towns as Austin, Mankato, Moorhead, Marshall, Winona, and St. Cloud. Party officials prominently identified with the Johnson-Humphrey position found themselves unceremoniously voted out of office. Many of these caucuses and the later conventions reverberated with personal denunciations, parliamentary manipulations, and ideological fervor reminiscent of the party's tumultuous clashes with its left wing twenty years earlier.

Finally, by the summer of 1968, when the DFL state convention wound up its business of completing a slate of delegates to the Democratic National Convention (Minnesota no longer had a presidential primary, so delegates were selected in convention) the relative strength of the two factions emerged with some clarity. "Administration loyalists" with aid from organized labor and party conservatives turned back their challengers from Rochester, Duluth, and the more rural areas of the 1st, 2nd, 6th, and 7th Congressional districts and retained decisive control of Minnesota's state DFL and of its Chicago-bound delegation. McCarthy forces petitioned in district court for redress of an alleged rural overrepresentation in the party's state convention apportionment formula, but this was denied. Humphrey was able to maintain a margin of 38½ convention votes to 13½ for his challenger.

The historic events of the Democratic National Convention need not be detailed here. Humphrey received the nomination on the first ballot. But it was a bittersweet victory, achieved against the background of bloody demonstrations in the streets of Chicago. And in the convention hall, as Humphrey received the cheers of his supporters and the congratulations of opponents like McGovern, there was a conspicuous absence: McCarthy pointedly declined to join his fellow Minnesotan on the platform and give him the endorsement traditionally offered by defeated candidates.

This act of independence and defiance was to have profound personal as well as political implications. For Humphrey and McCarthy and their masses of committed supporters it climaxed a historic confrontation that had severely disrupted friendships and long political associations. More than that, the consequences of this act may well have affected the outcome of a presidential election and thus the future course of the nation.

Though differing greatly in personality and style Hubert Humphrey and Gene McCarthy had been warm friends. For many years they had campaigned together and for each other. Jointly they had built Minnesota's DFL and helped write the party's platforms and programs. Since 1948 when both went to Washington, their associations had been close and on the major issues facing the nation their liberal voting records were nearly identical.

Naturally there had been tensions between these two highly intelligent and ambitious men, exacerbated by staff and factional rivalries, by problems of patronage and influence, and then in 1964 by rivalry for the vice-presidency. This was an office which, some observers believe, McCarthy very much desired for himself and for which he felt highly qualified; but unfortunately Humphrey also aspired to it and he believed himself clearly entitled to it on the basis of his seniority, national visibility, and legislative accomplishments — an assessment President Johnson apparently agreed with.

McCarthy's aloof stance after the 1968 convention did not help heal the factionalism in Minnesota's DFL. Many of McCarthy's backers felt hurt, betrayed, and deeply frustrated by what they viewed as the victory of the old politics over the new, of a "closed" over an "open" convention, of opportunism and reaction over principle and progress. For some of these people, Humphrey's failure to condemn Mayor Daley's police terror and to repudiate unequivocally Johnson's policies in Vietnam made unity nearly impossible. Only reluctantly did they accede to McCarthy's wishes that his name not be filed as an independent candidate. Humphrey's DFL supporters were bitter too. They had great difficulty in understanding what appeared to them the strangely enigmatic behavior of their senior senator — some called it arrogance. Failure to rally behind the national ticket seemed nearly "treasonable" for a man who had been a creator as much as a creature of the DFL and its tradition of endorsement discipline. Had he become a prisoner of his own rhetoric, was he simply anxious not to disappoint his youthful followers, was he looking to the future when he might wish to renew his crusade unsullied by compromises with the party establishment, or were these the actions of a man who cherished poetry more than power, lonely righteousness more than the cult of political pragmatism?

When Senator McCarthy finally did announce his formal support of Humphrey at a press conference, a week and a half before the election, the event and the nature of the endorsement had a certain anticlimactic quality. Disavowing a future role for himself in the party either as a senatorial candidate from Minnesota in 1970 or as a presidential candidate in 1972, he indicated that he "intended to vote for Vice-President Hubert Humphrey" and urged "those who have been waiting for this statement . . . to do the same." McCarthy emphasized that nothing in his endorsement was to be taken as forgiving or condoning "the things that happened both before Chicago and at Chicago."

On November 5, 1968, Hubert Humphrey brought Minnesota into his presidential column by an impressive margin: he won 807,122 votes to 620,687 for Richard M. Nixon and 66,948 for third-party candidate George Wallace. In one of the closest presidential races in American politics, Humphrey lost the United States presidency by a mere 500,000 votes out of a total of over 70 million. After a confused and very slow beginning from the depths of his party's "post-Chicago blues," and a consistently poor showing in early public opinion polls (the Gallup poll on September 29 showed Nixon 43 percent, Humphrey 28 percent, Wallace 21 percent), the Minnesotan had earned profound respect from political commentators and professionals for his great personal courage, boundless energy, and good humor despite hostile demonstrations, dispirited audiences, breakdowns in campaign logistics, and insufficient financial backing. Much has been written about a politician's true character revealing itself to the fullest in painful defeat. Humphrey demonstrated his quality in an emotional concession speech and a warm congratulatory telegram to President-elect Nixon which stressed his faith in the democratic process, gratitude for the efforts of his supporters, and a firm dedication to continued public service "to the cause of human rights, of peace, and to the betterment of man."

PARTY PATTERNS, ISSUES, AND LEADERS

Party prospects in the 1970's

In an intensely competitive political climate like Minnesota's prognostications are risky and often unrewarding. What are the political futures in the state of Humphrey and McCarthy for the DFL and of LeVander for the Republicans? All that can be said with some certainty is that their names must be listed among those to be followed with interest in the 1970's.

There are others. Both parties are rich in vigorous young leaders. For the Republicans there are the widely respected Congressmen Albert H. Quie and Clark MacGregor; the highly competent Attorney General Douglas Head, and the attractive Lieutenant Governor James B. Goetz. There are also the state auditor, William O'Brien, former Representative Emery G. Barrette, Judge Stephen Maxwell, and such fast rising senators as Wayne G. Popham of Minneapolis, William B. Dosland of Moorhead, and Kelly Gage of Mankato.

For the Democrats the highly effective young United States Senator Walter Mondale heads the list. Waiting in the wings of the state senate are Karl F. Grittner, Liberal minority leader; Nicholas D. Coleman, assistant minority leader; Wendell R. Anderson; and two young dentists from the range, the Perpich brothers, Dr. A. J. (Tony) and Dr. Rudolph G. Others are Martin O. Sabo, minority leader of the state house of representatives in the 1969 session; St. Paul's Mayor Tom Byrne, elected to his second term in 1968; the mayor of St. Cloud, Ed Henry, a political scientist from St. John's University, first elected in 1964; and Warren Spannaus, former state chairman.

As Minnesotans move into the politics of the 1970's this much seems clear. Party differences have begun to blur as Republicans and Democrats both address themselves constructively and very similarly to the urgent problems of the metropolitan areas and to the need for a rural renaissance (as Governor LeVander labeled it). Despite occasional differences in degree and method of approach, the platforms of the two parties, in often nearly identical words and phrases, stress the necessity for stimulating economic growth and business development, for

53

initiating action to protect consumers, for reorganizing state government, for safeguarding human rights, for assuring racial justice, for conserving natural resources, for controlling air and water pollution, for improving and advancing education, for strengthening health and welfare legislation, for easing the impact of the property tax on the elderly, for providing tax incentives to corporations willing to train the unskilled and economically handicapped, for assuring greater highway safety, and for improving public transportation.

Whether genuine progress can be made with sufficient speed and imagination to enlist the enthusiasm and support of the economically deprived, the socially disinherited, the uninvolved youth and blacks so that they too would wish to work within the framework of democratic institutions and processes and through such participation give to their lives a new sense of meaning — that also of course remains to be seen.

In a very real sense this may well represent the most difficult challenge that the decade ahead holds for Minnesota politics and politicians.

2

ELECTION LAW AND PARTY ORGANIZATION

Who may vote in Minnesota?

UNDER the constitution and laws of this state any 21-year-old United States citizen, native or naturalized for at least three months, unless convicted of a felony or declared mentally incompetent, is eligible to vote if he has resided for six months in Minnesota and for thirty days in his precinct. (The 1969 legislature approved for submission to the electorate in 1970 a constitutional amendment lowering the voting age to 19.) In presidential elections, anyone who has resided in the state less than six months but who is otherwise qualified to vote may cast ballots for presidential and vice-presidential candidates, but no others. In municipalities with a population of 10,000 or more, where registration is required, and in those communities under 10,000 which have voluntarily introduced a registration system, the voter must be properly registered before he can participate in elections. Residents of towns and cities where permanent registration systems are in effect make application to their respective city or town clerks (sometimes called commissioners of registration), and once entered on the rolls need not re-register unless they fail to vote once in four years or they change their place of residence. Those living in areas lacking such a system may be asked, if challenged, to take an oath that they are properly qualified as a condition for obtaining the ballot.

Minnesota law permits absentee voting by its residents who are in the armed services and by those unable to appear personally at the polls because of travel, religious holidays, or poor health.

Who may be a candidate for public office

With some exceptions, any qualified voter may also be a candidate for a state elective office. To run for governor or lieutenant governor, however, a person must be at least 25 years old and must have lived in Minnesota for at least one year preceding the election. Candidates for the United States Senate must be at least 30, have been a United States citizen for nine years, and be an inhabitant of the state; the minimum age for the national House of Representatives is 25, with a minimum citizenship requirement of seven years. Under a 1956 constitutional amendment those seeking office on the state bench (the supreme, district, and probate courts), and under state law those seeking municipal judgeships, must be attorneys at law.

Filing for office and the preparation of ballots

Persons seeking such statewide offices as governor, treasurer, or United States senator must file affidavits of candidacy with the secretary of state during a period fixed by law but not less than 56 nor more than 70 days before the state primary election. The same procedure applies to candidacy for the United States House of Representatives (except that in the 5th Congressional District the candidates must file with the Hennepin County auditor) and for the Minnesota legislature from districts not contained within a single county. Candidates to the legislature from one-county districts file with their county auditors, as do those seeking all county positions.

For all statewide and judicial offices, the filing fee is $100. Candidates for the United States House of Representatives and Senate pay fees of $100 and $150 respectively. The filing fee for the state legislature is $20; for county offices, $20; for offices in cities of the first class, $10, in cities of the second and third class, $5, in cities of the fourth class, $2. City charters, however, may provide for different filing fees from those given above.

When seeking offices that carry party designation, that is, the statewide nonjudicial and nonlegislative posts, candidates must indicate on their affidavit their party affiliation. According to state law this means merely that a candidate, unless voting for the first time, was "affiliated with his political party at the last general election . . . and [that] he voted for a majority of the candidates of the political party . . . and [that] he intends to so vote at the ensuing election." Minnesota does not provide for public registration of party membership; no formal evidence is required of the actual association of a candidate with the party organization; and no statement of party principle or philosophy is demanded. Thus an office-seeker's claim to party affiliation may have little or no substance.

Other and even graver abuses are encouraged by such lax filing procedures. Minnesotans — and the problem is by no means unique to this state — frequently witness the spectacle of last-minute filings by candidates whose motives are unworthy of the sanctity of the ballot and the public trust. Opportunists with no chance of winning and no genuine interest in political office are attracted by the free advertising and attention a public contest affords. Others unscrupulously use the filing privilege as a means of confusing the voters. More than once a party and its candidate have been plagued by the sudden emergence of a political unknown whose only recommendation is an ethnically typical name (in Minnesota, Johnson, Peterson, and Anderson carry a certain political magic) or a name identical to that of a major contender. Even when themselves innocent, these persons may have been inveigled into "stooge" roles by factions or leaders bent on rule or ruin tactics. In close contests such maneuvers can easily corrupt the vote.

There can be no defense of practices which mislead the electorate, disrupt the meaningful process of choice, and destroy the very essence of an orderly election. Various legislative proposals have been introduced from time to time in an effort to curb unethical candidacies, but none has as yet become law. One such bill, H.F. 1292, drawn in 1955 by Karl F. Grittner of St. Paul, then a state representative, would have required any candidate for office to file a special statement of "intent" with the secretary of state or the county auditor not more than 120 and not less than 50 days before the primary election. Additionally, it specified that candidates file a "nominating petition" signed by a stipulated percentage of voters, the percentage varying with the type of office. In the case of statewide offices these petitions would have to show genuine geographical distribution, bearing signatures from at least five congressional districts and with no more than 25 percent of the signatures originating in any one district. Supporters of H.F. 1292 and similar proposals contend that their admitted complexity would be well worth enduring if "stooge" and nuisance candidacies could thereby be reduced appreciably.

Minnesota law names city, village, and township clerks, county auditors, and the secretary of state as the key officials concerned with the supervision, preparation, and distribution of ballots, and charges them with the general administration of the election code. Recent statutes have increased the discretionary powers of these officials as regards the form, size, style, and type to be used in the actual printing of the ballot, but still governed by law are such matters as the position of the parties on the ballot, the rotation of names, use of sample ballots, colors, and the handling of ballot errors and corrections. White ballots, for instance, are to be used only for federal and statewide candidates, pink ballots for constitutional amendments, canary-colored ballots for county offices, and light green ones for town and village offices. To avoid confusion when the last names of candidates are spelled or pronounced similarly, the law permits as additional identification a reference in not more than three words to the person's office, his residence, or his occupation.

If the governing body of any municipality so decides, voting machines may be used instead of paper ballots. The type of machines used must be approved by a three-member state voting machine commission. The law also governs such matters as the arrangement of names on the ballot, provision for secrecy of the ballot, maintenance and custody of the machines, and voter assistance.

Minnesota has a long ballot, and her voters sometimes endure a tedious wait during the rush hours of an election day. To an already impressive list of federal and state officials are added, with slight variation from county to county (and from one election to another in the case of staggered-term offices), some fourteen or fifteen county positions: auditor, treasurer, register of deeds, clerk of court, sheriff, attorney, judge of probate, surveyor, coroner, court commissioner, superintendent of schools, Torrens examiner, and usually two or three of the five county commissioners. In municipal elections the length of the ballot varies from city to city. A Minneapolis voter at the 1969 general city election, for instance, was asked to vote on candidates for fourteen offices and on a charter amendment. In rural towns residents vote usually for one out of three supervisors, a clerk, a treasurer, an assessor, two justices of the peace, and two constables.

Primary and general elections

Minnesota now holds its primary elections for state and federal offices on the first Tuesday after the second Monday in September of each even-numbered year. The primary ballot includes all candidates for the United States Congress, for the state constitutional positions of governor, lieutenant governor, treasurer, auditor, secretary of state, and attorney general, for the office (created by statute) of public service commissioner (formerly railroad and warehouse commissioner), and for positions in the state legislature and state judiciary. (The 1959 legislature abolished the presidential preference primary law enacted in 1949. It had provided that candidates for nomination for the office of president could file either by affidavit or by a petition bearing the signatures of 100 voters of the party in each congressional district. The leadership of both parties had had embarrassing experiences during the life of the law — the Republicans in 1952, the Democrat-Farmer-Laborites in 1956.)

It was the muckrakers and reformers at the turn of the century who vehemently demanded public primaries conducted with secrecy, privacy, and opportunity for rank-and-file participation. In Minnesota the legislative history of the primary election begins with a law in 1899, which was applicable to Hennepin County only (city and county judicial candidates and candidates for school and park boards); in 1901 it was extended as a mandatory act throughout the state. In 1912 the legislature added state constitutional offices to the primary ballot. It is interesting to note that the 1912 measure grew out of political expedience: forces opposed to incumbent Governor Adolph O. Eberhart controlled the party convention and the governor's supporters believed that their candidate would fare better in a popular primary. After 1913 state legislators, county officials, and elected officials in cities of the first class also appeared on the primary ballot.

The consolidated primary ballot law was not adopted until 1933. Under its provisions the voter need not reveal his partisanship in any way, since a single ballot contains the names of all candidates for party-designated offices, arranged in separate columns according to party affiliation. The voter chooses among those who have filed for each office under his party's label the one he favors as that party's candidate for the ensuing general election; while he may of course abstain from voting for certain offices, he may not "split" his vote by wandering into the other party's set of candidates, on penalty of nullifying his entire ballot.

Along with this consolidated party ballot the voter also receives a primary ballot for non-party-designated offices. In such contests the two top-runners for each office become the winners of the primary election and the contestants in the ensuing general election. If there happen to be, for example, seven primary candidates for the non-party-designated position of representative to the state legislature from the 44th district, five of these seven will be eliminated while the two top vote-getters will go on to battle it out in November.

ELECTION LAW AND PARTY ORGANIZATION

The contests for party-designated offices are also usually between two candidates in the general election — one Republican meeting one DFL rival. However, participation by third parties and even by "lone wolves" is not precluded. Minnesota law enables groups too small to qualify as parties, and also individuals without any formal party support, to enter a general election by means of nominating petitions carrying a stipulated number of signatures, based on a percentage of the vote cast for the same office at the last general election. Write-in votes are also legal in general elections, and although some voters write in their own names, or Elizabeth Taylor's, a vital civil right is preserved thereby.

Elections and the counting of votes

As in most of the other states, general statewide elections are held the first Tuesday following the first Monday in November of each even-numbered year. Ballots for federal and state offices are cast and counted in approximately 3,800 precincts throughout the state. Polls remain open from 7:00 A.M. to 8:00 P.M.; notices giving the location of the precinct polling place and other pertinent information must be posted by the town, village, or city clerks at least fifteen days before both primary and general elections.

Municipal elections, primary and general, are customarily held at times governed by charter or general law. Annual village elections usually come on the first Tuesday after the first Monday in November or December, whereas most independent school district elections fall on the third Tuesday in May. Annual town meetings convene on the second Tuesday in March.

Election judges are appointed by municipal councils or county boards, with a minimum of three for each precinct. Each political party must be represented. In elections involving party-designated offices "the chairman of an authorized committee of each political party" may in writing present the name of a "challenger," who is then permitted to remain in the polling place. Either he or any one of the election judges may insist that persons with dubious qualifications who refuse to cooperate or decline to take an oath affirming the sufficiency of their qualifications be barred from voting under the terms of the election code.

How ballots are to be counted, how they are to be tallied, stored, and sealed, what is meant by a defective vote, and how election results are to be forwarded to the canvassing boards — all these operations are prescribed by state law. A county canvassing board includes the county auditor, the clerk of district court, two members from the county board, and the mayor of the most populous city. This board forwards to the secretary of state a certificate indicating the number of votes cast and counted and the results by precinct for each office, constitutional amendment, and other issue submitted to the voters. If a tie vote occurs the canvassing board may decide the outcome by lot; whenever election judges are suspected of error, the board may, if four-fifths of its members so vote, inspect a precinct's ballots. At the apex of the state election machinery stands the five-member State Canvassing Board, consisting of the secretary of state together with two district and two supreme court justices. This agency formally reports and certifies the official vote in a primary or general election.

Fair campaign practices laws

In order to ensure honest elections, the legislature under its police power has from time to time passed statutes regulating the conduct of campaigns. Political advertising and campaign literature must be properly labeled and identified; candidates and their supporters may not legally exert undue influence on voters or compel them to vote or to abstain from voting; no public or private promises may be given in exchange for a vote or as a promotional device; corporations are prohibited from making monetary contributions or from furnishing the "free service of [their] officers or employees." The purposes for which expenditures may be legally authorized are specified by law and include, among other items, office and hall rents, the printing of pamphlets, posters, handbills, and other campaign literature, filing fees, advertising expenses, and the candidate's personal travel, telephone, telegraph, and postal expenditures. Disbursements are allowable for expenses incurred by campaign organizers and committee members. Expenditure limits are fixed at $7,000 for gubernatorial candidates, at $3,500 for those seeking the other statewide constitutional offices, and at $800 and $600 for candidates to the state senate and state house of representatives respectively. Additionally allowable are expenditures equaling five cents per voter for that office in the previous election.

Obviously these sums, originally set in 1917, won't buy much of a campaign today. As a matter of fact they have been circumvented legally and effectively, as for example by the activities of so-called volunteer or political committees. Enjoying freedom from fixed statutory limits on expenditures and receipts, such committees may, according to judicial interpretations and rulings by various attorneys general, collect and spend funds to the extent of their ambition and ability. Volunteer committees and their candidates thus acquire influence and financial power at the expense of the party organizations, whose fiscal activities are so much more carefully restricted. The major parties and most of their candidates have long favored raising the statutory limits to a more realistic level.

In Florida, candidates may spend money without restriction but they must make periodic public accounting of the source and disposition of campaign funds. In addition Florida requires that all financial transactions pass through the hands of a publicly announced campaign treasurer (selected by the candidate himself), that all contributions be kept in a special bank account, and that no payments be made by anyone without a formal voucher submitted to the campaign treasurer for his approval. The Florida experiment, while only one of various approaches to the tremendously complex interplay of money and politics, has been viewed with much interest by students of campaign finance in Minnesota as well as other states.

POLITICS IN MINNESOTA

Parties and party organizations

Although only 21 of the approximately 32,500 local, state, and federal offices on Minnesota ballots carry party designation, these 21 include such important posts as United States senator, United States representative, state governor, other state constitutional officers, and (in presidential years) president and vice-president.

These are the prizes for which the parties struggle as they reeruit candidates, fight campaigns, write platforms, arouse the enthusiasm of their own supporters, and attempt to make converts from the opposition and from those who classify themselves as "independents." Despite the impressive role they play, there is not a single word in either the state or the federal constitution referring to political parties and their functions. Courts in Minnesota and in other states, however, have held the organization of political parties to be an inherent right of citizenship. Like any other right it is not absolute, but may under certain circumstances be made subject to legislative control.

Under Minnesota law a political group in order to be recognized as a legitimate party must operate a statewide organization and must have presented in every county one or more candidates who polled at least 5 percent of the total vote cast at the last general election. Parties may also obtain a place on the primary election ballot by a petition to the county auditor containing signatures numbering at least 5 percent of the total vote cast at the last general election in the county.

The law forbids the theft of names of already existing parties, nor may any part of a current party label be appropriated by any other party or candidate. In view of Minnesota's history of third parties and of hyphenated parties which have resulted from the marriage of once-separate factions, this concern for the integrity of party labels is no mere technicality. Without legal prohibitions, a splinter group or a dissident candidate could gain votes, or at least confuse and mislead the electorate, by using such appellations as "Democratic-Labor," "Farmer-Labor-Republican," or simply "Democratic" alone. In the 1953 legislative session a quiet effort was made by some anti-Humphrey forces to amend the law and permit appropriation of another party's name. What this would mean in a closely fought contest, if for example a Democratic ticket were placed alongside a Democratic-Farmer-Labor ticket, is not too difficult to imagine. Fortunately for party "regulars" the bill died in the closing hours of the session.

Under the terms of the 1968 election code final legal authority over the internal affairs of each political party is lodged in the state convention it must hold at least once every general election year. These conventions may be considered the highest legislative assemblies of the parties. Between sessions of the convention, "subject to the control of the state convention," as the law puts it, the state central committee is invested by the election code with power over a party's affairs.

Within their broad statutory framework parties work out their own constitutions, promulgate rules, and perform all the other tasks required of self-governing organizations. Despite important differences in outlook and perhaps even in composition, the organizations of the major parties are very similar.

Precinct caucus and county, district, and state conventions

To the average citizen, the precinct or township caucus is the most significant of the several party assemblies. Here, on the lowest stratum in the party pyramid, is the arena where the rank and file of party membership — the perhaps ten or fifteen voters in the neighborhood (out of perhaps fifty) who consider themselves politically active — meet at least once every other year in order to conduct important party business. At the caucus, delegates to county conventions are chosen, the precinct's own committee officers are elected, party policies and personalities are discussed, rejected, and endorsed.

Thus action taken on the precinct level carries decisive implications for the party as a whole. Yet Minnesota belongs to that group of states which demand only the most minimal and subjective tests as prerequisites to caucus participation. A voter's statement that he supported, voted with, or affiliated with the party in the past, that he agrees with its principles as stated in the party constitution, and that he promises future support — only such generalized affirmations are required of him. And since his support may well have been confined to the privacy of the polling booth and the secret ballot, external verification is difficult. If challenged, however, an individual's right to participate may be put to a vote by the precinct caucus.

The law has singled out these primary party meetings for careful attention — and with good reason, since precinct "raiding," when carried out systematically and by design, can put an entire party in danger of seizure from within by elements completely antagonistic to its established principles. A political party, it should be remembered, is something more than a mere private club transacting private business; a party's choice of candidates and its endorsement of policies have ramifications for the entire body politic. Hence the legislature is rightfully concerned that the precinct caucus should be convened and conducted with fairness and with certain procedural safeguards.

The law prescribes that the "call" (the formal document sent out by the county chairman of the party announcing the precinct caucuses) must indicate (in addition to the date, time, and location) the number of delegates to be elected, the nature of the business to be transacted, and the names of the precinct and county chairmen. Space is provided on the back of the call for the names and addresses of the delegates elected to the county conventions. This facilitates the issuing of credentials by the county chairman to newly elected delegates.

Precinct caucus and precinct organization have properly been called the backbone of party structure. If the local party workers slacken their efforts or if they incorrectly reflect public sentiment, campaign goals are jeopardized and elections may be lost. On the other hand an active local organization can do much to bring new recruits and resources to the party. Many an election has been won or lost by the degree of enthusiasm with which precinct workers distributed literature, placed posters, collected money, organized house-to-house canvasses, sponsored coffee parties, conducted telephone drives, and performed the myriad of other tasks without which campaigns are rarely successful. For best results, of course, precinct activities must be integrated into the county and statewide campaign strategy so as to avoid duplication of effort.

In the cities all the precincts located within a "ward" — a somewhat flexible area which in Minneapolis constitutes an aldermanic district — may wish to form a ward club. Joint party educational programs and socials can often further the effectiveness of the local organization and help in its campaign tasks.

Generally, precinct delegates make up the membership of county conventions, county delegates the congressional district conventions, and county and district delegates the state convention. In conventions at the county level and above, both of the major parties determine the number of delegates from each lower unit by apportionment formulas, based usually on party vote in the precinct, county, or district at the last election. Certain party officials, however, become delegates ex officio.

To give their party greater organizational continuity and stability, Republicans made a number of important constitutional changes in 1959. Instead of meeting biennially as specified earlier, county and district conventions are directed to assemble every year, and district conventions and county conventions may elect their officers in odd-numbered years. The regular DFL conventions all meet only in election years, although there may be "extraordinary" conventions called at other times. In the metropolitan areas the DFL now selects its state convention delegates from the assemblies in the state senatorial districts.

The county, district, and state conventions follow the precinct caucuses at two- or three-week intervals; their structure and order of business are somewhat similar. After the customary invocations, speeches of welcome, and announcements comes the first important issue: the seating of delegates. This is accomplished by adopting the report of the Credentials Committee, a group which along with several other appointed committees (as for example Platform, Rules, Resolutions, Nominations, Constitution, Endorsements, Arrangements) has convened in advance of the convention itself. Given party harmony, the work of the Credentials Committee is little more than a routine scrutiny of the delegates' certificates; but on occasion seats are bitterly contested, especially if irregularities occurred at lower conventions or if intraparty disputes have produced rival slates with opposing claims of legitimacy. In such cases the faction dominating the Credentials Committee may in effect steer the outcome of the convention itself.

Perhaps second in significance to the Credentials Committee is the Committee on Rules. Its report, when adopted by the convention, governs the agenda or order of business, defines the procedure for formal voting and other parliamentary practice (as for example the number and length of seconding speeches, or the allocation of voting power in case of absences in a delegation), stipulates the circumstances under which a roll call may be demanded, sets the quorum required for floor business, and — unless provided for specifically in the party's state constitution — decides the conditions under which the convention may endorse candidates for public office.

Once properly organized, the convention gets down to business, for it must elect convention officers and party officers, choose delegates for the next higher convention, perhaps make amendments to the party constitution, and come to decisions regarding the party's platform and policy. Often its most touchy business concerns the endorsement of candidates.

Heated debates over endorsement have given conventions of the DFL party an air of suspense and drama, as well as considerable publicity. The issue is joined, as we saw in Chapter 1, between those in favor of pre-primary party endorsement of particular candidates and those opposed. Proponents of pre-primary endorsement stress the need for party unity in the primaries; they argue that financial and organizational resources can be used to better advantage in fighting "the enemy" than in family quarrels; they reason that early endorsements produce strong, responsible, balanced party tickets committed to the support of party platform and principle; they claim too that campaigns are most effective when all members of the ticket support each other and reinforce each other's appeal. Voters, they argue, will be less open to exploitation by high-pressure personalities, "beauty" contests, stooge candidacies, and irresponsible appeals when they have the counsel of professionals who have looked over the field and approved the most reliable and promising candidates. Since serious misjudgments in endorsement are very injurious to the party's chances in the general election, the party leaders are likely to be very careful. And after all, they conclude, there still remains the public primary, at which voters may turn down party recommendations and thus register grass-roots protest when it appears that the "regulars" have made a mistake.

Opponents of pre-primary endorsement rest their case squarely on what they insist is the heart and spirit of the primary as a device, designed by reformers and independents, to take the power to nominate candidates from the hands of bosses, machines, and party organizations, and return it to the rank and file, who can then vote for their candidates rather than for those chosen for them by the "professionals." Through pre-primary endorsements, parties *tell* the voter for whom to vote rather than *ask* him whom he wants as his nominee. Who is better entitled to voice the sentiments of the party than the majority of individual members who cast their votes in the secrecy of the primary? And should not the nonconforming political figure who is out of favor with the party palace guard have an opportunity to put the strength of his personality and conviction to the test of rank-and-file vote? They might decide he can best minister to party ills.

These arguments were put forth in much this form in 1966 when DFL Governor Rolvaag had the endorsement wrested away by Lieutenant Governor Keith at the party's state convention. As we have seen, Rolvaag decided to contest the convention's decision by carrying the struggle into the primary, where his campaign centered on the theme "Let the people decide." In the arguments offered by each side to support its own position, that primary stands as a classic example of the struggle between those favoring pre-primary endorsement and those opposing it.

DFL leaders such as Hubert Humphrey and Orville Freeman have always considered the pre-primary endorsement a *sine qua non* for building a responsible and effective party program, for conducting successful campaigns whether the office is state or federal, legislative or executive. Despite bitter internal struggles and slow beginnings, the DFL party has been generally successful in utilizing the pre-primary endorsement, for since its fusion in 1944 it has been able to carry nearly four out of five endorsed candidates through the primary elections, the 1966 state campaign being a notable exception.

The tradition against official pre-primary endorsements is much stronger in the Republican party. In part because of rural fears of urban-dominated party councils, perhaps in part because of the influence of strong personalities irrevocably opposed to party endorsement, various moves to adopt this practice suffered repeated defeats during the 1940's and 1950's. However, in 1959 the party took a step in the direction of pre-primary endorsement when it amended its constitution to permit such endorsements. Under the present provision, a convention may by vote of 60 percent of the total delegate strength (rather than by the two-thirds vote required in the DFL) give pre-primary endorsement to candidates for any public office. However, endorsement for any such public office carries with it the resources of the party organization only if made at the convention which represents the entire electorate for that office (state convention endorsement for statewide offices, county convention endorsement for countywide offices, etc.). Endorsement made at levels lower than the entire electorate for that office are considered to be merely expressions of "sentiment." The party's state constitution also provides that "when more than one such candidate is nominated for endorsement, none of them shall be voted upon separately and the candidacy of all shall be submitted on each ballot."

State central and executive committees

During the intervals between state conventions each party functions through its central and executive committees.

Meeting two or more times a year, the central committee of each party has between 200 and 300 members and includes the major leadership of the party. Among the members are the state executive officers (chairman, chairwoman, vice-chairmen, vice-chairwomen, secretary, and treasurer), the corresponding executive officers of county and district organizations, the national committeeman and committeewoman, representatives of the party's nominees for major state and federal offices, county delegations (in addition to county officers), and the executive officers of such auxiliaries as the Young Republican League, Federation of College Republican Clubs, Federation of Women's Republican Clubs, and the Young Democratic-Farmer-Labor clubs. Delegates may be sent to represent those state constitutional offices currently held by the party. The DFL admits delegates sent by the Liberal members of the Minnesota legislature, and in addition it seats its immediate past chairman and chairwoman. The Republicans allow the larger counties additional votes on the central committee, based on a formula of one extra vote per 5,000 votes for governor in the preceding election. Thus, for example, on the basis of the 1968 election results Hennepin County was entitled to 33 votes, Ramsey County to 14, and St. Louis County to 5.

In both parties the executive committee is a smaller group of usually 30 to 65 persons, among them the state executive officers, the national committeeman and committeewoman, the eight district chairmen and chairwomen, other party leaders appointed by the chairman and chairwoman or elected at large by party groups at the county, district, and state levels, and (for the Republicans) the governor and United States senators (if, of course, of that party). Meeting as often as once a month, the executive committee carries out the policies of the state convention and state central committee; its chairman, who also chairs the central committee, is known as the chairman of the party. Among other duties the executive committee maintains a party headquarters where the party's day-to-day activities in public relations, finance, and organization are handled by a small full-time staff. In recent years the work of political parties in Minnesota and elsewhere has become so heavy as to require the services of an executive secretary. Such a salaried official is appointed by the state chairman with the advice and consent of the executive or central committee.

In a politically competitive state like Minnesota state chairmen and executive directors face constant challenge. Organizational and publicity problems must be solved or elections will be lost. Inactive county and district groups must be rebuilt, family quarrels smoothed over, new members recruited, finances kept on a solid footing, and so on. Precinct, county, and district efforts must be integrated into the state strategy. Membership lists and voter registration must be kept up to date, money collected, patronage problems settled, disaffected officers replaced, vacancies filled. The party executive must meanwhile get favorable newspaper coverage for his party's activities and must keep the opposition's moves under scrutiny and criticism. Whether the legislature is in session or not, whether the party is in office or not, these party executives must meet an unending series of demands for leadership and conciliation, for information and favor, for assistance and counsel.

Among the Republican chairmen of the past several decades R. C. Radabaugh, Bernard LeVander, P. K. Peterson, and John Hartle are especially remembered for their long service and influence on the party. All were connected with the Stassen administrations: Radabaugh as Stassen's campaign manager, LeVander as state director of social welfare, Hartle as a Stassen spokesman in the state house of representatives, and Peterson (elected a public service commissioner in 1966) as a state legislator. Ed Viehman, a business associate of Dan C. Gainey, an influential Republican from Owatonna, was chosen in January of 1959 after the election of his predecessor, Ancher Nelsen, to Congress. Viehman, who had managed successfully two congressional campaigns for Albert H. Quie of the 1st District, reflected the more conservative thought in the party. He was succeeded after his death by Robert Forsythe, a prominent attorney. After serving with distinction for several years, Forsythe stepped down to run against Walter Mondale for his Senate seat. George Thiss assumed the chairmanship in 1966 upon Forsythe's resignation. Prominent Republican chairwomen of the same era include Marge Howard of Excelsior, Rhoda Lund of Minneapolis, Kay Harmon of St. Paul, Mrs. H. G. Dillingham of St. Paul, and Mrs. Mark G. Brataas of Rochester.

Orville L. Freeman, state DFL chairman from 1948 to 1950, was succeeded by Karl F. Rolvaag. He, in turn, was followed by Ray Hemenway of Albert Lea when the DFL swept into office in 1954 and Freeman became governor, Rolvaag lieutenant governor. Hemenway was succeeded by Adrian Winkel of St. Paul, who preceded George Farr, chairman from 1960 to 1967. Warren Spannaus, former state assistant attorney general, was elected in 1967 to fill the vacancy left by Farr's resignation. When Spannaus resigned in 1969, Richard Moe became chairman.

Working closely with the Humphrey-Freeman leadership in the late 1940's and early 1950's was state chairwoman Dorothy Houston Jacobson of Minneapolis. Like Humphrey a former political science professor, Mrs. Jacobson (later to become assistant secretary of agriculture for international affairs in the Kennedy administration) was long identified with the cooperative movement and with liberal politics; she was a major tactician in the struggle against the left-wing forces in the DFL in 1948; and she became respected perhaps more than any other single person in the party as a consultant on policy to Governor Freeman. She was succeeded as chairwoman by Anne Vetter (1956–58), Geri Joseph (1958–60), Evelyn Malone (1960–62), Pat St. Angelo (1962–63), Betty Kane (1963–68), and Koryne

Horbal (elected in 1968). Among highly competent executive secretaries two men in particular stand out for their effectiveness, Herbert O. Johnson (GOP) and James Pederson (DFL).

Special projects and party finance

If voters feel that their political party is a mere patronage mill, or if they feel that it keeps watch over them with the unfriendly and dictatorial mien of the "Big Brother" in Orwell's *1984*, they will sooner or later lose their loyalty and enthusiasm. The party will then sicken and elections will be lost. Accordingly, a party must recognize its responsibility to serve as a forum for mature deliberation of meaningful issues. For example, two district organizations might jointly sponsor a regional conference to deal with agriculture, labor, health, or leadership training. When the legislature is in session, party workshops might study and criticize current issues and bills. The DFL has organized legislative tours in which several Liberal members of the state house and senate visit a number of communities in every congressional district in the state discussing what the legislature has done in the past session and what might be done in the upcoming session. For a "The People Speak" conference several years ago the Republicans sent out invitations to hundreds of groups and organizations throughout the state, soliciting their opinions on such issues as agriculture, conservation, civil rights, education, foreign affairs, human welfare, small business, industry, and labor. To aid in the preparation of its platform, the state GOP has organized "task forces" which examine each topic to be dealt with in the party's platform. Among the 45 major topics covered in 1968 were metropolitan affairs, civil disorder, education, air and water pollution, underdeveloped nations, and Vietnam and Southeast Asia.

For any such special projects and, of course, on a much larger scale, for election campaigns, political parties must have financial resources. Because literature, staff, newsletters, radio and television time, newspaper advertising, and other campaign requirements cost enormously, no party or candidate has ever felt that there were sufficient funds to do the job. Much of the party's energy must go into raising money. First, each party through its finance committee and finance director seeks out individuals and organizations friendly to its program and candidates; second, there are money-raising rallies such as the Republicans' annual $100 a plate dinner and the DFL's annual Jefferson-Jackson Day dinner; third, there are the less formal "Fun Fests," "Bean Feeds," "Neighbor to Neighbor" and "Friends and Neighbors" drives, appreciation banquets, and so forth. The DFL makes collections through its sustaining membership plan, under which a member may contribute as little as $1.00 per month; $2.50 or more per month gives him an annual subscription to the nationwide *Democrat* and also one ticket to the $25 a plate Jefferson-Jackson Day dinner. The Republicans, too, use a pledge and sustaining-fund system.

Such are some of the methods for raising money, but what of the sources of funds? Large contributors still pay the major share of party expenses. Fund raisers on both the state and national levels agree that approximately 90 percent of the money comes from not more than 1 percent of the population, that about 60 percent of the amount contributed comes in denominations of $500 or over, and only 20 percent in sums under $100. Forty percent of the DFL's yearly revenue is derived from the sustaining fund, 29 percent from dinners, 24 percent from galas and special projects, and 7 percent miscellaneous; nearly 100 percent of the state GOP's money comes from their Neighbor to Neighbor drive and their $100 a plate dinner. With campaign funds an object of suspicion and disdain in American politics, evoking memories of "bought" elections and "kept" candidates, political parties in Minnesota and other states must find new ways to convince the average citizen that his financial support, as a material accompaniment to his political convictions, is a practical and perhaps an ethical imperative.

The question, then, is how to broaden the base of campaign financing by getting the thousands of average citizens who have never made a contribution in the past to give financial support to the party of their choice and to back the campaigns, candidates, and causes in which they believe. DFL leader Byron G. Allen was instrumental in two pioneering experiments in Minnesota that have been used to attack this problem.

The first of these resulted in a law (passed in 1955) permitting any individual (corporations excepted) to deduct from his taxable net income contributions of up to $100 to political parties, candidates, or groups. Party officials may claim sums up to $1,000, depending upon the office, as credits against taxable net income. Candidates for any public office may deduct from their gross income specified amounts ranging up to $5,000 for a United States senator or state governor.

The second experiment was encouraged by then Senators Thye and Humphrey, by the national committee chairmen of both major political parties, by various Washington political figures, by the editor of the *Washington Post,* and locally by the Advertising Council of Alexandria, Minnesota, and the *Park Region Echo,* the weekly newspaper of that city. In May 1956 Alexandria was the site of a bipartisan mass appeal for political funds; during three evenings teams of Democratic and Republican canvassers who went jointly from door to door approached 1,000 voters (the population was 6,300) and collected $1,200. Seventy-six percent of those approached made a contribution. This wide response indicated the possibilities for broadening the base of campaign contributions; it also showed that in a small town, at least, the voters are not particularly eager to be publicly identified with a party. It was reported that only 20 persons chose to specify that their contributions go to a particular party.

State-national party links

A conspicuous feature of the American party system is the looseness of party organization on the national level. Neither the Republican nor the Democratic party is nationally much more than an association or confederation of autonomous state units. Subject of course to state and federal statutory limitations, the final authority over the internal affairs of Minnesota parties remains within the state and in the parties' own state conventions. Each party's national committee serves as a sort of liaison council during the interim between national conventions, preparing for these conventions, coordinating campaign activities, supervising the party's Washington administrative headquarters, and assisting with patronage clearances whenever the party's candidate is in the White House. Since so much of the party's organizational work and power rests, however, on the state level, the national committeemen and committeewomen sent by Minnesota and the other states might be thought of as ambassadors speaking for the state party organizations by whom they are elected and to whom they are responsible.

Although meeting regularly only three or four times a year, the members of the parties' national committees perform essential functions. When a Republican occupies the White House, members of the Republican National Committee are consulted or expect to be consulted about patronage, campaign tactics, and party finance. On occasion they may assist in persuading a reluctant congressman to see things the administration way. During a Democratic administration the Democratic National Committee serves similarly as a liaison between Washington and the state organizations.

Mrs. Ione Hunt of Montevideo, long-time DFL party leader and member of the Democratic National Advisory Council, operative during the Eisenhower years, succeeded to the post of national committeewoman when Mrs. Eugenie Anderson of Red Wing was appointed by President Truman as this nation's first woman ambassador to Denmark in 1949. Mrs. Geri Joseph became the state's Democratic national committeewoman in 1960. Gerald W. Heaney succeeded Byron G. Allen in 1955 when Allen was appointed state commissioner of agriculture; Heaney later became a United States circuit court judge. Ray Hemenway became national committeeman in 1960; he was succeeded by Congressman John Blatnik.

On the Republican side Roy E. Dunn, veteran member of the

Minnesota house and its long-time majority leader, served as
national committeeman for sixteen years. "Mr. Republican,"
as his friends liked to call him, was a strong Taft supporter
and a frequent vigorous opponent of Stassen's views. Mrs. Elizabeth Heffelfinger of Wayzata, at one time a Stassen supporter
and a ten-year national committeewoman, along with George
W. Etzell of Clarissa (Dunn's successor in 1952), played an
effective part in the Republican national organization. Etzell
was chairman of the Rules Committee, while Mrs. Heffelfinger
chaired the Committee on Arrangements for the 1956 Republican National Convention and was secretary to the executive
committee of the National Committee. Mrs. Rhoda Lund became national committeewoman in 1960.

In a presidential election year the national convention is the
last and highest in the sequence of party assemblies which
began at the grass roots with precinct caucuses. Such a convention is of course a major undertaking, involving not only
immediately practical considerations — feeding and housing
thousands of delegates and visitors, arranging for press, radio,
and television coverage, furnishing headquarters space and staff
for the would-be candidates — but also the maintaining of a
community of purpose in the face of strenuous rivalries, and
the presentation, to millions of Americans who act as the audi-
ence, of a viable party "image."

Even more than at the state level, the make-up of the
national preconvention committees has tremendous consequences for the party as a whole. Presidential nominations and
the party platform may well depend on the seating or rejection
of certain delegations, on the establishment of certain rules of
order, on the ideological fervor of certain committees. It is the
national committee and its chairman who stand close to the
sources of power and who influence appointments to the Rules
and Platform and Credentials committees.

Its nominees chosen and its platform written, the national
convention adjourns and party activity reverts to the state
and local level. Both parties' national committee members set

themselves to the task of coordinating their state campaigns with the nationwide design. Among other things, they make every effort to have their state included in the speaking itinerary of the nominees. More because of its location and its representativeness than because of its electoral weight, Minnesota has heard a number of major campaign addresses in the past. Harry Truman made a belligerent indictment of the 80th Congress at St. Paul in 1948. Also in 1948 Henry Wallace condemned both major parties and called for a new political alignment during a speech in Minneapolis. Both Stevenson and Eisenhower delivered important policy statements on agriculture at Kasson, Minnesota, in 1956. In the 1960's most of the major candidates visited the state.

To make maximum capital of such speeches, to use all other means to rally the doubtful and keep the already loyal active — this is the job of precinct, county, district, and state party organizations, in Minnesota as in the other states.

3

A NONPARTISAN PARTISAN LEGISLATURE

WITH the single exception of Nebraska's unicameral legislature, Minnesota's is the only state legislature whose membership is elected on a ballot without designation of political party. Party designation was dropped in 1913 largely as the result of a parliamentary struggle between the "drys" and the "wets" in which the opponents of prohibition working with liquor interests exploited sentiments within the legislature that were strongly critical of party machines and boss control. One must remember that this was the era of progressivism, when parties were disdained and political independence was extolled, and when it was hoped that direct political action by the people (through such means as the initiative, referendum, recall, and direct primary) would lead to more responsible government.

Political history since the early part of this century has thrown some doubt on the efficacy of these devices; it no longer seems axiomatic that the weakening of political parties serves the ends of good government. Already in 1913 voices of doubt were raised. After the Minnesota senate had added the nonpartisan feature to the primary election law, commentator Charles B. Cheney, a supporter of nonpartisanship on the local level, wrote in the *Minneapolis Journal* that "the Minnesota plan throws the door open to the nominations of the liquor and other interests as they find it easy to juggle the contests once they have degenerated into mere personal struggle."

The debate over the desirability or undesirability of party labels for legislators has since then been one of the constants in Minnesota politics. The problem becomes ever more acute as the increasing power of the modern legislature affects larger numbers of people over wider areas of their lives.

Legislators and legislative organizations

Minnesota with its 135 representatives and 67 senators has the largest senate and eleventh largest house in the nation. Representatives stand for election every two years, senators every four (in nonpresidential election years). They receive salaries ranking well up among the upper fourth of those paid to legislators throughout the United States.

It may be of interest to note certain characteristics of the members of the 1967 legislature. The occupations of the legislators varied somewhat between the two houses. In the senate 35.8 percent were lawyers, 10.5 percent farmers, and 34.3 percent businessmen. In the house 24.4 percent were lawyers, 20.0 percent farmers, and 27.3 percent businessmen. ("Business" here includes insurance and real estate.) In age there was no notable difference between the two chambers; the average age in the house was 48.4 years, in the senate 51.0.

Table 1. Percentage of Legislators with Given Previous
Experience in the Legislature

No. of Terms	1893	1909	1925	1935	1951	1959	1967
One previous term or none							
Senate	74	15	13	22	29	60	64
House	82	54	54	19	38	26	43
Three or more previous terms							
Senate	21	59	81	49	54	24	19
House	5	27	32	53	47	41	33

Source: From data in William P. Tucker, "Characteristics of State Legislators," *Social Science*, 30:94–98 (April 1955), p. 96, and the *Minnesota Legislative Manual (1967–68)*, pp. 31–85.

The extent of the legislators' previous experience is shown in Table 1. It is quite apparent that since 1951 important changes have occurred in the membership of the senate. In that year more than half of its members had served three or more terms; in 1967 more than half had served no more than one previous term. Thus there was in the 1967 session a concentration of experience and power in a relatively small group of senators with long seniority.

In addition to considering and acting on bills, a modern state legislature must discharge a multitude of other duties in connection with its role as agent of "check and balance" for the executive and judicial branches and for local government units. These include such actions as confirming gubernatorial appointments, determining legislative contests, proposing amendments to the constitution, conducting hearings and investigations, and providing for interim legislative committees and commissions. Before it can do all this, the legislature must of course bring itself into parliamentary order by electing presiding officers, selecting committee members, determining rules, and agreeing to a calendar. Obviously a group of several dozen legislators would be unable to function unless it employed some kind of "team" structure permitting men of similar interests or aims to act as a unit, at least in formal aspects of the legislative "game." Instead of the Republican-Democratic bifurcation characteristic of other states, the Minnesota house and senate divide themselves into Liberal and Conservative caucuses. Nominations are made by each caucus for the key positions of speaker of the house and president pro tem of the senate.

The group which can command a majority of legislators' votes and so elect its candidates in either the senate or the house is known as the majority caucus in that chamber. This is where much of the legislative power resides, for in Minnesota the winner takes all. The winning caucus through its election of the majority leader and speaker or president pro tem controls the chairmanship of legislative committees and through the Rules Committee directs the general flow of legislative business. The parliamentary powers of the speaker of the house are particularly extensive: he appoints all the standing committees of that body, "signs all acts, addresses, joint resolutions, writs, warrants, and subpoenas," prepares schedules of committee meetings, designates the chief sergeant at arms, and refers bills, after their first reading, to appropriate committees.

Senior members of the majority caucus chair such key committees as Finance (senate) or Appropriations (house), Taxes, Rules, Highways, Education, Labor, Public Welfare, Judiciary, Civil Administration and Metropolitan Affairs, and Agriculture. Here bills are shaped into final form, hearings are held that focus attention and support, and administrative departments attempt to justify their programs and budgets.

In the past four decades, the Conservatives have been in firm control of the senate. The Liberals have controlled the house only in 1933, 1937, 1955, 1957, 1959, and 1961.

Conservatives holding influential positions of floor and committee leadership in recent decades have been such men as the following: Roy E. Dunn, majority leader in the house for nine of the sixteen sessions in which he served — longer than anyone else in the history of the state; Lloyd L. Duxbury, Jr., speaker of the house since 1963; Aubrey W. Dirlam, majority leader of the house since 1963; Richard W. Fitzsimmons, house Appropriations Committee chairman; Rodney N. Searle and Roy Schulz, both active in the house in the field of education; Charles N. Orr, majority leader in the senate for five special and nine regular sessions; A. J. Rockne, "watchdog of the treasury" and twenty-year chairman of the senate Finance Committee; Donald O. Wright, a veteran of more than 30 years' service and chairman of the senate Tax Committee since 1951; and Gordon Rosenmeier, chairman of the senate Judiciary Committee and highly influential member of the senate Conservative caucus since 1941 — critics and supporters of his agree there are few men who bring to their positions the practical intelligence, analytical mind, parliamentary skill, and legal competence of the senator from Little Falls. These men have fought hard and effectively against executive and legislative proposals that seemed to them "too costly," "too liberal," "too untried," or "too dangerous." Some of them skirmished with Christianson, Stassen, Andersen, and LeVander; some campaigned against the

83

Youngdahl program; most fought vigorously Farmer-Labor or DFL administrations. Some opposed any measures strengthening the governorship or centralizing the administration; others objected to tax increases and the adoption of an income tax; some rejected expansion of government services and government regulation; not a few of them viewed with alarm the rise of organized labor and the intervention of government in new socioeconomic areas. All have stood for the constitution as framed, for the rights of property and the sanctity of contracts, for the preservation of a government which in their judgment best assures continuation of the traditions of American freedom and individualism. And in their continued re-election they have seen proof that their constituents deem their positions worthy of support.

In the senate the citadel of present Conservative leadership is the Committee on Committees headed by Rosenmeier. On this committee sit the chairmen of such other vital committees as Finance, Taxes and Tax Laws, General Legislation, Judiciary, Labor, Civil Administration and Metropolitan Affairs, Public Welfare, Rules and Legislative Expense, and Education. The chairmen making up this committee in the 1967 session were all Conservatives. They represented six congressional districts, had an average age of 64, and had served an average of twenty years in the senate. Another Conservative bastion, likewise restricted to the majority caucus, is the Committee on Rules and Legislative Expense chaired by majority leader Stanley W. Holmquist. Though other important committees are not altogether closed to the minority caucus, that group is allotted less than proportional representation. For example, the Liberals in 1967 held 6 of the 23 seats on the Judiciary Committee, 7 of 27 on Civil Administration and Metropolitan Affairs, and 9 of 24 on the less-strategic Game and Fish Committee. This "closed" committee system is a perennial point of dispute between the two caucuses, as is the prerogative now held by the Conservatives of making all committee appointments, including those from Liberal ranks. In recent years, particularly under the leadership of Senator Holmquist, efforts have been made to meet these Liberal criticisms, and to give that caucus more equitable representation and more of a voice in the determination of the Liberal complement for each of the committees.

In the Conservative-controlled house in 1967 the Liberals were excluded from the Rules Committee but held 9 of 33 seats on Appropriations and a similar quota on the Tax Committee — both of which approach proportional representation for the Liberals, since they held 42 of 135 seats. This more generous arrangement is at least in part due to a 1957 rules amendment (sponsored by the Liberals) which directs the speaker to "give due consideration" to committee preferences of the minority caucus "with the end in view of attaining a proportionate representation on such committees for the minority group."

Liberals have bitterly criticized the Conservatives in control of the senate for dragging their heels on reform measures, for blocking or slowing down legislative action considered essential by the Liberals. The split control of the legislature between 1955 and 1961 was a source of anguished frustration for the Liberals and their supporters. Yet, whatever inefficiency or inaction resulted from such an arrangement, Minnesotans apparently preferred such diffusion of legislative power. They apparently wanted not only the customary check and balance of the executive, legislative, and judicial departments upon one another, but the check of house against senate and senate against house possible when each chamber of the legislature is dominated by a different caucus.

For example, on June 9, 1957, the "Minnesota Poll" of the *Minneapolis Tribune* provided evidence on this point when it reported responses to the following: "In the 1957 session, the Conservative members were in control of the state senate, while the Liberal members were in control of the lower house. Do you think this kind of divided control is a good thing or a bad thing for the state?" Those indicating they thought it a good thing were more than twice as many as those who thought it a bad thing:

	Total	Men	Women
It's a good thing	45%	49%	40%
It's a bad thing	20	21	18
No difference	1	2	less than 1%
No opinion	34	28	42

Further proof that Minnesotans endorsed the idea that one house of the legislature ought to check the other might be seen in another survey taken by the "Minnesota Poll," one published on November 22, 1964. This was the issue as stated in the Poll: "Some people say that if both houses of the legislature must be organized on a population basis, then Minnesota ought to have a one-house legislature. Do you agree or disagree with that?" In response the following breakdown of opinion was noted:

	Total	Men	Women
Agree	25%	28%	23%
Disagree	49	54	44
Other, no opinion	26	18	33

Contrasts in the caucuses

The Liberal and Conservative caucuses of the 1967 legislature showed some differences in the geographic distribution of their strength. As shown in Table 2, although 69 percent of the total house membership was Conservative, 71 percent of the rural and 82 percent of the suburban legislators were Conservatives. At the same time, although Liberals made up only 31 percent of the total house membership, they constituted nearly 50 percent of all "core-city" legislators, those from Minneapolis and St. Paul. Similarly, in the senate Conservatives made up 67 percent of the entire body but 92 percent of all suburban and 70 percent of all rural legislators; Liberals, 33 percent of the total senate, made up 47 percent of all core-city senators. Thus it is apparent that the Conservatives were particularly strong in the suburban areas, while the Liberals drew their greatest strength from the core-city urban areas.

Tables 3 and 4 show interesting age and occupational contrasts. In the senate, 64 percent of the Liberals were under 50

Table 2. Geographical Distribution of Legislators

Area	Number			Percentage	
	Total	Liberals	Conservatives	Liberals	Conservatives
Senate					
All	67	22	45	33	67
Core-city [a]	15	7	8	47	53
Suburban [b]	12	1	11	8	92
Rural with city of 25,000 [c]	6	2	4	25	75
Mixed [d]	3	2	1	67	33
Rural [e]	27	8	19	30	70
Rural-suburban [f] ..	4	2	2	50	50
House					
All	135	42	93	31	69
Core-city	35	17	18	49	51
Suburban	28	5	23	18	82
Rural with city of 25,000	2	1	1	50	50
Mixed	4	0	4	0	100
Rural	66	19	47	29	71

[a] Core-city: those districts within the cities of Minneapolis and St. Paul.

[b] Suburban: those districts in Hennepin County not in the city of Minneapolis; those districts in Ramsey County not in the city of St. Paul; those districts in the counties of Washington, Dakota, and Anoka.

[c] Rural with a city of 25,000 or more: those districts which contain a city with between 25,000 and 50,000 inhabitants located within an otherwise rural district.

[d] Mixed: those districts which are in part core-city, in part suburban, and in part rural — the Duluth–St. Louis County districts.

[e] Rural: all those districts not included in categories a–d and f.

[f] Rural-suburban: those districts which are in part made up of Twin Cities suburbs and in part of rural areas. The House has no districts in this classification.

Table 3. Ages of Minnesota Legislators in the 1967 Session

Age	Senate				House			
	Conservatives		Liberals		Conservatives		Liberals	
	No.	%	No.	%	No.	%	No.	%
30 and under	0	0	0	0	2	2	1	2
31–40	8	18	8	37	26	29	5	12
41–50	10	22	6	27	32	34	14	33
51–60	13	29	4	18	14	15	18	43
61–70	12	27	2	9	14	15	4	10
71 and above	2	4	2	9	5	5	0	0

while only 40 percent of the Conservatives were. House Liberals appeared to be more "middle-aged" than did house Conservatives. Seventy-six percent of the Liberals were between the ages of 41 and 60, while 31 percent of house Conservatives were 40 or under and 20 percent were 61 or older. In both the house and senate there were proportionately more lawyers, businessmen, and farmers among Conservatives than among the Liberals.

Table 4. Occupations of Minnesota Legislators in the 1967 Session

Occupation	Senate				House			
	Liberals		Conservatives		Liberals		Conservatives	
	No.	%	No.	%	No.	%	No.	%
Lawyer	6	27.3	18	40.0	7	16.8	26	27.9
Businessman	6	27.3	18	40.0	10	23.8	26	27.9
Farmer	1	4.5	6	13.4	7	16.8	25	26.8
Educator	3	13.7	1	2.2	5	11.9	3	3.0
Doctor	3	13.7	0	0.0	2	4.7	0	0.0
Insurance man ..	2	9.0	1	2.2	2	4.7	6	6.4
Cooperatives employee	1	4.5	1	2.2	0	0.0	0	0.0
Housewife	0	0.0	0	0.0	2	4.7	0	0.0
Newspaper editor..	0	0.0	0	0.0	0	0.0	1	1.0
Engineer	0	0.0	0	0.0	0	0.0	2	2.0
Draftsman	0	0.0	0	0.0	0	0.0	1	1.0
Union official	0	0.0	0	0.0	3	7.1	0	0.0
Right-of-way negotiator	0	0.0	0	0.0	1	2.4	0	0.0
Skilled laborer ..	0	0.0	0	0.0	3	7.1	0	0.0
Policeman	0	0.0	0	0.0	0	0.0	1	1.0
Minister	0	0.0	0	0.0	0	0.0	1	1.0
Retired	0	0.0	0	0.0	0	0.0	2	2.0

The political parties and the caucuses

As already indicated, Minnesota legislators are elected without designation on the ballot of party membership or affiliation. For organizational purposes they group themselves into Conservative and Liberal caucuses — again without any explicit reference to party. A question often asked is how "partisan" is this nonpartisan body? One experienced political commentator, Ralph Fjelstad, after analyzing the voting during the 1953 session, was satisfied that Minnesota legislators tend to follow their factional commitments in much the same way that lawmakers in a partisan legislature respect their party lines. But are these legislators influenced by *party* lines as well as *caucus* lines?

The question cannot be answered simply, for the situation is a complex one. And it is not the same with respect to the two major parties.

Liberals in both legislative chambers have been frank to acknowledge their family ties with the Democratic-Farmer-Labor party. Most of the Liberals in the legislature openly identify themselves with the DFL; many of them have served as county or district committeemen. Moreover, the DFL constitution provides explicitly for representation from the Liberal caucuses on the party's state central and executive committees. As nonvoting members these caucus delegates attend the party's state conventions as well.

Such interrelationship of party and caucus has not always existed. During the Olson and Benson regimes important administrative proposals failed to become law because of faulty liaison and lack of cohesion, even during the two sessions of 1933 and 1937 when the house at least was nominally controlled by Liberals elected with Farmer-Laborite support. There were several reasons why the party, even in the days of its large popular majorities, lacked effective control of the legislature. In the first place, the Farmer-Laborites were unable to translate their heavy 1932 and 1936 majorities into senatorial strength because all members of the upper house are elected in "off years," not in presidential election years such as 1932 and 1936. Secondly, in the absence of party designation or pre-primary endorsement, voters were by no means sure of candidates' positions on major issues. A proof of this was the election of Conservative legislators from districts otherwise heavily Farmer-Laborite. A biographer of the Farmer-Labor party, Arthur Naftalin, has suggested a third reason: "During a reform era, in the absence of party discipline, the nonpartisanly elected legislator, left to his own judgment, finds Conservative affiliation an easier matter because it requires no positive avowal on his part in support of a definite program, whereas affiliation with the Liberals requires a rigorous understanding of, or at least sympathy for, a program of reform."

Today's DFL organization has resolved not to repeat the mistakes of the Farmer-Laborites. Accordingly, it gives the weight of party endorsement to approved candidates for the legislature, prints their names on its sample ballots, and sends its leaders to their districts to speak on their behalf. The DFL also has developed methods of recruiting new candidates; its precinct, ward, and county organizations are urged to interview liberally inclined farmers, businessmen, and professional men, to encourage their interest in politics, and to support them actively if they choose to run for legislative office. Organized labor groups and Liberals already in the legislature have aided in these efforts, which since the early 1950's have brought considerable talent into the Liberal caucuses, as for example Joseph E. Karth (four-term member of the house before his election in 1958 as United States representative from the 4th District), Donald Fraser (state senator from 1954 to 1962 before his election to Congress from the 5th District), Karl Grittner (who served in the house from 1952 to 1958 before election to the state senate), Nicholas Coleman (first elected to the senate in 1962), and Martin Sabo (first elected to the house in 1960).

Although at one time Conservatives in the legislature were reluctant to identify with the Republican party, approximately 85 percent of the house Conservatives are now active Republicans. Some Conservative leaders in the house in recent years have held top-level positions in the party. Roy E. Dunn was national committeeman; John A. Hartle, former speaker and long-time majority leader, was state chairman; P. K. Peterson also served as state chairman. The list of Republican congressmen and state officials who served their political apprenticeship as Conservatives in the legislature is a long one, including in the recent period Ancher Nelsen, Odin Langen, George Mac-Kinnon, Albert H. Quie, and John Zwach.

Among senate Conservatives, 75 percent of whom acknowledge active participation in the Republican party, Donald O.

Wright was a delegate to the 1940 Republican National Convention; Stanley W. Holmquist served as a district chairman; Walter J. Franz was treasurer of the state central committee in 1954; and John Tracy Anderson was chairman of St. Paul's 12th Ward GOP Club. Other senators active in Republican politics are Clifton Parks, Robert J. Brown, and Roy W. Holsten.

Party workers among house Conservatives in the 1967 session included Walter K. Klaus (former 2nd District chairman), Robert G. Dunn (member of Mille Lacs County Republican Committee), Otto Bang (former chairman of the Edina Republican Committee), Lyall A. Schwarzkopf (Hennepin County GOP chairman), Arlan Stangeland (former chairman of the Wilkin County Republican party), and Ernest Schafer (chairman of the Renville County Republican party). Other state representatives involved in the Republican party organization at various levels are Rodney N. Searle, F. Gordon Wright, and Gary W. Flakne.

Despite this demonstrable interrelationship between party and caucus, a basic question remains: Do members of the nominally nonpartisan caucuses actually *vote* along party lines? In other words, are the caucuses in effect agents or representatives of their respective parties, regardless of what they are in theory?

Partial answers can be offered from an analysis of voting records on a number of proposals advocated in the platforms of both major parties. The issues are these: a constitutional convention for the purpose of bringing the state's 1857 charter up to date (Table 5); party designation of state legislators (Table 6); an "equal opportunities" or fair employment practices law (Table 7), and reapportionment.

The three tables show that the Liberals conform more closely to the party position than do the Conservatives. Although neither caucus achieved unanimity at any time, each showed a characteristic "center of gravity" suggestive of the tensions and alignments within it; and on these issues at least, the in-

Table 5. Roll Call Votes in the House (1949) and Senate (1955) on the Proposal to Call a Convention for Constitutional Revision [a]

Direction of Vote	House (1949)				Senate (1955)			
	Conservatives (N = 86)		Liberals (N = 44)		Conservatives (N = 48)		Liberals (N = 19)	
	No.	%	No.	%	No.	%	No.	%
Pro	46	54	34	77	11	23	16	84
Con	31	37	9	20	37	77	3	16

Source: Minnesota House, H.F. 810, April 8, 1949, p. 1889; Minnesota Senate, S.F. 23, March 15, 1955, p. 797.

[a] Because of absenteeism and nonvoting, percentages do not add to 100. There was in addition one house member listed as an "Independent" whose vote is not tabulated here.

Table 6. Roll Call Votes in the House (1951–63) on Proposals to Establish Party Designation of State Legislators [a]

Session and Direction of Vote	Conservatives [b]		Liberals [c]	
	No.	%	No.	%
1951 session				
Pro	28	32	25	60
Con	48	55	11	26
1953 session				
Pro	52	61	36	78
Con	28	33	8	17
1955 session				
Pro	19	29	43	65
Con	45	69	23	35
1957 session				
Pro	37	61	58	83
Con	21	34	11	16
1959 session				
Pro	9	15	52	72
Con	47	80	18	25
1963 session [d]				
Pro	32	40	45	83
Con	48	59	7	13

Source: Minnesota House, H.F. 9, February 13, 1951, pp. 406–7; H.F. 329, March 13, 1953, p. 1010; H.F. 12, February 15, 1955, p. 492; H.F. 41, February 15, 1957, pp. 446–47; H.F. 61, February 3, 1959, p. 15; H.F. 1099 (vote on motion to make H.F. 1099 a Special Order), April 23, 1963.

[a] Because of absenteeism and nonvoting, the percentages do not add to 100.

[b] The total number of Conservatives in 1951 was 88; in 1953, 85; in 1955, 65; in 1957, 61; in 1959, 59; in 1963, 81. (In 1951 one representative is listed as an "Independent.")

[c] The total number of Liberals in 1951 was 42; in 1953, 46; in 1955, 66; in 1957, 70; in 1959, 72; in 1963, 54.

[d] A vote to place a bill on special order requires a two-thirds majority.

Table 7. Roll Call Votes in the House (1951–55) on Proposals for a
Fair Employment Practices Law [a]

Session and Direction of Vote	Conservatives [b]		Liberals [c]	
	No.	%	No.	%
1951 session				
Pro	42	48	33	79
Con	43	49	5	12
1953 session				
Pro	41	48	40	87
Con	39	46	5	11
1955 session				
Pro	33	51	63	97
Con	28	43	2	3

Source: Minnesota House, H.F. 74, March 29, 1951, pp. 1520–21; H.F. 622, April 18, 1953, p. 2377; H.F. 778, April 7, 1955, pp. 1789–99.

[a] Because of absenteeism and nonvoting, the percentages do not add to 100.

[b] The total number of Conservatives in 1951 was 88; in 1953, 85; in 1955, 65. (In 1951 one representative is listed as an "Independent.")

[c] The total number of Liberals in 1951 was 42; in 1953, 46; in 1955, 66.

dependence of the Conservative caucus from the Republican party platform cannot be easily denied.

Although fair employment practices and the constitutional convention have declined as pressing issues, party designation still comes up every legislative session. But the last time that party designation came to a vote in any form on the floor of the legislature was in 1963, and then only on parliamentary maneuvers to remove the bill from committee. In 1965 and 1967 various bills proposing party designation were deeply buried in committee, in both the house and the senate. Some of them were so bogged down that hearings were not even held on them, nor were they ever voted upon. They simply did not come up for action, even in committee.

If we use the issue of reapportionment for legislative districts (also long demanded in both party platforms) as a further test case, the results are similar. During the ten years preceding the 1959 reapportionment act, numerous such bills were introduced in every session, few of which reached the roll-call stage. One that did reach a vote, the Bergerud-Gillen bill, passed the house in 1957, 68 to 61, with 64 percent of the Conservatives and only 31 percent of the Liberals opposing it. Some of the

93

other reapportionment bills would have avoided cutting rural representation by increasing membership in one house or the other or by changing the basis of representation in one house to area instead of population. But the Bergerud-Gillen bill in essence directed the carrying out of the constitutional mandate to reapportion on the basis of population. Of those in both caucuses voting against the measure, 83 percent came from districts that were overrepresented in the legislature by approximately 20 percent.

What all of this illustrates, some contend, is less the independence of the Conservative caucus from the Republican platform than the dependence of this caucus on its rural sources of power. This may well be true, for all four of the issues studied touch on rural-urban conflicts, and negative votes in all four instances reflect possible rural interests. For example, a new constitution might be resisted because it would presumably provide for reapportionment. Reapportionment in the 1960's has in fact shifted power to the metropolitan areas while taking away from rural Minnesota the overrepresentation it once enjoyed. Even fair employment practices legislation becomes a sectional issue, for the rural economy depends in part on the use of seasonal labor in harvesting and canning.

A 1966 research study by Larry Frederickson of Macalester College dealing with the extent of caucus cohesion in the Minnesota legislature revealed some interesting findings. In analyzing 107 roll calls in the 1961 session and 93 roll calls in the 1963 session, he found that on votes where an absolute majority of one caucus was opposed by an absolute majority of the other (more than two-thirds of the roll calls in both sessions were unanimous), caucus cohesion was greater on issues reflecting national conservative-liberal alignments (power of organized labor, health and welfare) and lowest on issues such as those dealing with state administrative and judicial questions, taxes, highways, local government, and rules and procedures. He also observed that among the most "caucus-conscious" DFLers were attorneys, labor leaders, and representatives from urban districts, while among Conservatives the most "caucus-conscious" were farmers, businessmen, and representatives from rural GOP districts. Those who deviated most from caucus lines in the DFL were legislators from marginal areas of party strength (most rural) while among Republicans the deviates represented mostly suburban districts and were the chronologically young members of the group.

The case against party designation

Certainly the influence of rural interests may be seen in the arguments advanced in support of the tradition of nonpartisanship in the legislature. Such veteran senators as Gordon Rosenmeier and Daniel S. Feidt have argued vigorously that a Conservative (they prefer the label Independent) has no responsibility or accountability except that leading directly back to his own constituents. They have asserted that unlike Congress, a state legislature is concerned mainly with law enforcement, conservation, education, elections, local government, daylight saving time, liquor control, water safety, highway construction, teacher retirement plans, trucking permits, and many other issues on which public opinion is divided not primarily along party lines, but according to geographic — rural versus urban — or economic interests. In representing his constituents' opinions, then, the legislator may well be forced into deviation from any and all party platforms.

These Independents conceive of a legislative caucus as a voluntary and perhaps temporary collaboration of like-minded persons for parliamentary purposes; by no means is this caucus to be construed as the arm, agent, or creature of a political party. Basically, the position of the supporters of nonpartisanship rests on their suspicion of, if not downright antagonism to, centralized party organizations, which they consider dominated by "bosses" and "machines." Implied here is belief in a disproportionate influence of metropolitan and labor interests on party councils. They fear too that gubernatorial domination of the legislature, as an outgrowth of "party discipline," would jeopardize the

95

traditional separation-of-powers principle which has made American politics safe and cautious rather than efficient and overhasty.

Another argument stems from the doctrine of legislative individuality and independence: to some any party discipline smacks of a collectivism to which they are philosophically and temperamentally opposed. Their attitude is reminiscent of Edmund Burke's famous speech to his Bristol constituency affirming that "[a legislator's] unbiased opinion, his mature judgment, his enlightened conscience, he ought not to sacrifice to you, to any man . . ." This is not to imply, however, that the Independents are unable or unwilling to act in concert or to form "cabals" to block legislation inimical to them.

Finally, the Independents maintain that public opinion in Minnesota backs them up, and that there is no majority sentiment in favor of party designation or any of the other devices of legislative partisanship. The result of a number of public opinion surveys conducted by the "Minnesota Poll" have generally confirmed this contention.

The Poll posed its question on this subject in some such form as the following: "Some people think that members of the state legislature in Minnesota should be elected under political party labels — that is, as Democratic-Farmer-Laborites or as Republicans — rather than on a no-party basis as they are now. Do you think legislators should be elected under party labels or not?" While sentiment for party designation increased over fourfold between 1945 and 1969, only three times (in 1954, 1964, and 1969) did a majority favor it:

Date	For Party Designation
March 1945	14%
February 1946	46
March 1947	39
July 1954	53
February 1955	38
April 1957	36
December 1958	40

A NONPARTISAN PARTISAN LEGISLATURE

Arguments for party designation of the legislature

Despite the lack of strong popular support, a number of groups are currently agitating for a return to party designation of legislators — among them some important Republicans as well as spokesmen for the DFL; the Farmers Union; the League of Women Voters; and a number of labor unions.

They have various reasons for advocating party labels, but their arguments can be summarized as follows: (1) A party-designated legislature would be better equipped to resist the special interests and local interests which now influence policy in a disproportionate and often undesirable manner. (2) A modern state government faces tremendous obligations in the fields of social, labor, and welfare legislation; to finance its new operations it must devise adequate but equitable taxation. On issues such as these, which affect all geographic areas and all economic groups, it is unrealistic to maintain that there can be no party position. On the contrary it is only the party system, representing as it does the broader coalitions of sectional and group interests, which can achieve social justice. (3) Reform platforms and proposals have little chance of enactment unless the governor can count on legislative support. The degree of executive-legislative teamwork necessary to implement election promises cannot be obtained without party designation. (4) The absence of party designation has in effect clothed with tremendous power a very small group of very conservative legislators elected from small constituencies or from districts where the voters know little about them. These men have been in a position to thwart Republican and Democratic governors elected by popular mandate, and their "invisible government" — so the argument runs — leads to cynical and irresponsible politics. In dealing with the issue of nonpartisanship in a study of the Minnesota legislature, political scientist

Charles Adrian concluded that despite the imperfections of the American political party, "It is the best vehicle available for insuring responsibility of the lawmaker to the people." (5) If legislators were elected with party labels, the precinct, ward, and county organizations would be revitalized and their work made more meaningful. There would be more interest in recruiting and supporting candidates, and increased participation in primary and general elections would result.

The reapportionment struggle

The Minnesota state legislature, acting under threat of federal court order, passed a reapportionment act in 1959, based on the 1950 census, effective January 1, 1962.

The 1960 census, however, revealed serious inequities in the new apportionment. In the senate the largest district was over four times the size of the smallest. In the house, this ratio of largest to smallest was seven to one. It was found that 39.1 percent of the 1960 population could elect a majority in the senate, and 35 percent could do so in the house.

In early June 1964, a group of nine officials from suburban areas, including Congressman Clark MacGregor, filed suit in federal court to compel the legislature to redistrict before the September 8 primary elections. Later, they changed their request to specify January 1, 1966, as the date by which reapportionment had to be accomplished.

In December, the federal district court ruled the 1959 apportionment to be in violation of the equal protection clause of the 14th Amendment to the United States Constitution, and therefore invalid, and warned the legislature to take action or face further court proceeding. Moreover, in line with then-recent United States Supreme Court decisions, the court declared that both houses of the legislature, not merely the house of representatives, must be apportioned on the basis of population.

In July 1964, Governor Rolvaag appointed seventeen persons

to serve on a bipartisan reapportionment commission. This move was strongly criticized by Conservatives in the legislature, who protested Rolvaag's failure to select high-ranking Conservatives in the legislature to balance the ranking DFL participants. The commission submitted its report in December 1964. It called for a shift of 17 seats (5 in the senate and 12 in the house) to the Twin Cities suburban area. This report satisfied the plaintiffs in the original lawsuit but drew sharp criticism from Conservative legislators as being unduly favorable to the DFL and as being an invasion of what they felt to be solely a legislative concern — reapportionment.

The 1965 session of the legislature then passed a bill shifting 5 senate and 10 house seats to the Twin Cities suburbs. The bill was vetoed by Governor Rolvaag, who claimed that the bill was unconstitutional and "intolerably deficient in population equality." After nine legislators unsuccessfully attempted to contest in the Minnesota courts Rolvaag's authority to veto a reapportionment act, the legislature, meeting in special session, passed a second reapportionment bill. This bill, too, was vetoed by the governor, who attacked it for not providing "a fair and adequate system of legislative districting" and for "creating grotesquely-shaped gerrymanders." Finally the legislature, continuing to meet in special session — the calling of which itself was the subject of much bitter public debate — on May 18, 1965, passed yet a third reapportionment act (shifting 5½ senate seats and 11 house seats from outstate into the suburbs), which was signed into law by the governor on May 21, thus ending one of the most controversial and interesting chapters in Minnesota political history. (See Figure 4.)

While urban voters gained political strength in both senate and house, it was to be essentially Conservatives rather than Liberals who seemed to benefit most from the reapportionment. This was particularly true for the house in the 1966 election: all of the new suburban seats were captured by legislators affiliating with the Conservative caucus.

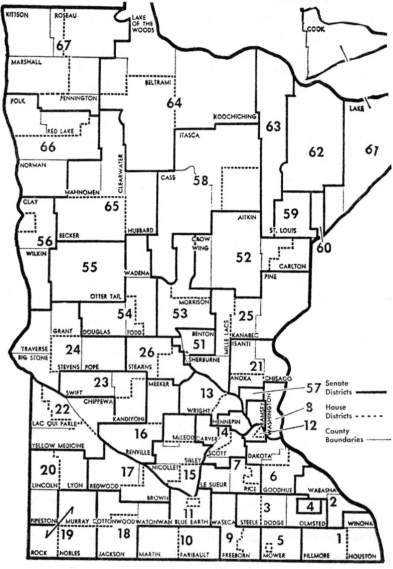

Figure 4. Legislative Districts Established under the
Reapportionment Act of 1966

A NONPARTISAN PARTISAN LEGISLATURE

Some basic governmental and political issues, pending and future

The legislature seems destined to figure prominently in most of the current or future "great debates" confronting the people of Minnesota. The issue of party designation, already discussed at some length, is one.

Another is constitutional revision. Should the legislature now call a constitutional convention to revise or rewrite Minnesota's century-old basic charter, or should the lawmakers continue to rely on piecemeal amendment? Those who favor the convention method argue that because of their complexity and their interdependence with existing articles, many reforms can be effected only through a revision of the entire constitution. Among the reforms mentioned frequently are these: a provision for the initiative and the referendum, a short ballot for state executive officers (with its consequent expansion of gubernatorial appointive powers), the unfreezing of dedicated funds, the creation of mandatory reapportionment machinery, and the scheduling of annual instead of biennial legislative sessions. It seems to many cheaper, more democratic, and more efficient to deal with such problems all at once in a convention dedicated to that task, rather than to work for the passage of separate amendments, some of which would necessarily be drafted in haste, insufficiently debated, and inadequately presented to the public.

Opponents of the convention method emphasize the greater safety and practicality of the piecemeal approach. They point, too, to the important reforms already achieved by various amendments. Since 1956 alone, entire articles have been rewritten covering such subjects as highways, judiciary, local government, term of office for the chief executive officers, and succession to the governorship in case of death or incapacity. It is admitted, of course, that amendments, particularly those of a more complicated or technical nature, have suffered a high mortality rate at the hands of Minnesota voters, and that the stiff requirement for passage (a majority of all votes cast at that election rather than a mere majority of all those voting on the question) makes ratification difficult. However, the rejection rate has decreased significantly during the last twenty years. In the period 1948–58 one out of every two amendments submitted to the voters won public approval at the polls, and in the period 1960–68, 73 percent of all proposed amendments passed, whereas 67.5 percent of the amendments submitted between 1898 and 1946 failed to pass. No doubt the pressures for reform stemming from population increase and from postwar socioeconomic conditions helped to expose some of the inadequacies of the existing constitution; perhaps the threat of a constitutional convention, should the habitual rejection of amendments frustrate necessary reforms, also served as a stimulus.

Another important issue is taxation — an area of legislative activity bristling with problems, as has already been indicated. Who should pay, and how much? Upon what kinds of property or economic activity should the major burden of state and local taxation rest? What kinds of exemptions and tax credits ought to be worked into the state's sales tax system? Is the sales tax a replacement for other sources of revenue or a supplement to them? Can and should taxes on farm and business inventories be reduced or eliminated? How can tax assessment and tax equalization procedures be reformed? How can citizens of the state be guaranteed a more equitable distribution of tax funds so that there will be proper and adequate revenue sources for local units as well as for the state government, with its ever-increasing needs? How does Minnesota's tax climate compare with that of other states? How can business and industry be attracted, retained, and encouraged to expand while at the same time required to pay their fair share of the tax burden?

Legislative reorganization and reform is of course of particular concern to the legislators. Should the number of committees be reduced, to permit the harassed lawmaker to devote more time to major issues? Should more formal and detailed journals and records be kept of legislative and committee proceedings?

(This could affect future campaigns, by making possible a more explicit comparison of a candidate's promises with his post-election actions.) Should new rules be adopted to facilitate the return to the floor of bills pigeonholed or buried in hostile committees? Should the minority caucus be given the right to name its own representatives to legislative committees? Should legislator-attorneys be prohibited from representing private clients before state executive or regulatory agencies during the period between sessions? To what extent should lobbies be regulated? Should the legislature be freed from its present fiscal straitjacket, so that it might exercise greater power over all the revenues of the state?

There are a number of current problems relating to the executive branch. Although the Reorganization Act of 1968 constitutes a significant step in the direction of strengthening the governorship, there remain such questions as these: Should the governor be granted wide appointive powers similar to those enjoyed by the president of the United States? These new powers might enable the state chief executive to choose (with the advice and consent of the senate) such officials as the secretary of state, the treasurer, and perhaps even the attorney general, thereby building a strong and integrated cabinet to replace the present slate of constitutional officers each individually responsible to the electorate. Should the office of state auditor be redefined as that of legislative watchdog over executive expenditures (by analogy with the United States comptroller general)? Should the Public Service Commission (formerly known as the Railroad and Warehouse Commission) become a gubernatorially appointed rather than a popularly elected body? Or should the members of this commission be designated by the legislature, as is the present procedure with regard to the University of Minnesota's Board of Regents? To what precise extent should the governor be permitted to consolidate into a few major departments the many functions now performed by a plethora of separate agencies, bureaus, commissions, boards, and divisions? How can the lines of authority and accountability in the state's central administration be clarified and strengthened? Would further executive reorganization unduly strengthen the governorship, thereby jeopardizing the separation of power doctrine? Would further executive consolidation together with the shortened ballot injure political parties, who depend on a large slate of offices to evoke public interest and to permit compromise and coalition among their internal factions?

A challenge of intensifying concern to the legislature is that of metropolitan population increase, particularly in and around the Twin Cities. The Metropolitan Planning Commission (which was replaced in 1967 by the Metropolitan Council) established by the 1957 legislature to provide "advisory metropolitan planning service for the area consisting of Anoka, Dakota, Hennepin, Ramsey, and Washington counties" (Carver and Scott counties joined later) submitted estimates of great significance to both state and local governments. By 1980, according to the commission's figures, this metropolitan area alone will be obliged to provide for 600,000 more residents, for 250,000 more jobs, for 175,000 more dwelling units, for 140 more schools, for 900 new miles of streets and highways, for a 120-million-gallon daily increase in water consumption, and for 700 more policemen and firemen. The enormous financial burdens and other problems of "megalopolitan" growth may force the legislature into new statutory as well as merely advisory roles, especially as these new population concentrations affect the tax base, the pattern of revenue expenditures, the balance of rural against urban interests, and other statewide issues.

There are many other issues that will also come before the legislature. But these indicate the scope and complexity of legislative business in the future.

4

LOBBIES BEFORE THE LEGISLATURE

The how and why of lobbies

M OST people are confused, if not downright misinformed, about the role of lobbies in a democratic society. The subject is an especially pertinent one for Minnesotans, since their state's very powerful non-party-designated legislature may well attract more than its share of lobbyists.

Lobbies are not unique to the democratic form of government, but are better detected and studied in such an environment. In an authoritarian context the same pressures are exerted in a carefully concealed, mysterious, subterranean fashion. In the United States, on the other hand, lobbying is part and parcel of our political tradition. By inference it is sanctioned in the 1st Amendment to the Constitution, which safeguards "the right of peaceful assembly and of petition for redress of grievances"; Article I of the Minnesota constitution declares that "Government is instituted for the security, benefit and protection of the people, in whom all political power is inherent, together with the right to alter, modify or reform such government, whenever the public good may require it."

A lobby may be defined as an interest group concerned primarily with the promotion or modification of, or opposition to, legislation and governmental regulations. As such, its activities may impinge on the legislature, on committees and individual members thereof, or on the executive branch together with its bureaus and agencies, or on regulatory commissions charged with the application to particular cases of extant but broadly stated laws — indeed, at various times, on all of these.

A lobby is born out of the specialized, homogeneous needs of a particular occupational or social group. Doctors, lawyers, farmers, teachers, businessmen, bankers, and working people in general usually lack the time or the know-how to keep the legislative process under constant scrutiny or to influence it toward their group's advantage. Consequently such people may found associations to represent them on Capitol Hill and express their wishes. These associations — call them "lobbies" if you will — may employ full-time or part-time staffs, may operate continuously or *ad hoc,* may actually vote some of their own membership into political office. (As one magazine writer put it, referring somewhat wistfully to the Minnesota situation, "You don't need lobbyists here; this legislature has its own built-in lobby.") Though they usually exert direct pressure on the legislature and other policy-making bodies, some lobbies pursue their objectives more indirectly by working on the home constituency of a senator or representative. This is often very effective just before a primary or general election.

Like the Constitution itself, lobbies can be termed "party blind." They work within, between, and across party and caucus lines. With a more deeply committed membership, better financing, and clearer goals, they are frequently more than a match for a much larger but much more heterogeneous political party.

Good and bad lobbies

Lobbies have been praised and condemned, investigated and restricted. They have been called "the third house of the legislature" and blamed for immoral pressures and undercover operations. The federal government and thirty-eight of the states require lobbyists to register, indicating their employers and their objectives (though not in Minnesota); in some states, they must also file financial reports.

In their defense it can be argued that lobbies supply lawmakers with necessary information, that they serve to check and balance each other, that they enunciate the legitimate objectives of particular professional or socioeconomic groupings, and that with their specialized backgrounds they can assess the beneficial or deleterious effects of proposed laws and regulations. However, nobody will claim that lobbying is an unmixed blessing. Lobbyists sometimes speak only for themselves and the bureaucratic officialdom of their organization rather than for the rank-and-file membership, whose only function is to watch apathetically from the sidelines. In a larger sense lobbying may be injurious to a society, for wherever lobbying is rampant the unorganized and inarticulate interests (as for example the long-suffering consumer) are especially apt to be ignored.

Then there is the question of lobbying tactics. Many of these are legitimate, useful, and ingenious. Some — such as threats, bribes, and "deals" — are explicitly illegal and punishable. Other lobby strategies are in the border areas of political morality: it is one thing to persuade a legislator with facts and reasons, and quite another to assail him with distorted statistics, juggled graphs, exaggerated propaganda, and deliberate misinformation. Those who defend lobbying point out that the meretricious claims of one pressure group are likely to be refuted by its competitors, and that a free-for-all on Capitol Hill is evidence of a healthy body politic. With each lobby claiming that what is good for it is good for all, democratic theory presumes the emergence of a majority consensus on what is actually in the interest of all the people. Those holding this somewhat over-optimistic view argue that if all interests, organized and unorganized, are allowed to interact openly and freely, more justice than injustice will prevail in the end.

Lobbying, then — its functions, merits, abuses — is a controversial and complicated issue best studied in terms of particular cases. Out of the literally hundreds of groups and associations which converge on the state capitol during each legislative session, six have been selected for a closer look. These six organizations, of course, perform many services in addition to lobbying — educational, economic, social — but for the purposes of this

chapter they will be studied chiefly in terms of their impact on
the legislature.

The Minnesota League of Women Voters

Established in 1920, the Minnesota League of Women Voters
is a powerful civic reform group with approximately 5,500 members distributed throughout the state but heavily concentrated
in St. Paul, Minneapolis, and Duluth. According to its own
publications, "The League is nonpartisan. It takes action in
support of or in opposition to selected governmental issues, but
does not support or oppose . . . candidates . . . or . . . political parties." It urges its members to work in the party of their
choice and to support issues and candidates conducive to good
government on the local, state, and national levels. League
programs have included campaigns to get out the vote, meetings
with candidates, legislative workshops, and election campaign
schools. Among League publications (most of them pamphlets
designed for study and discussion groups) are *You Are the
Government* (1948, 1959), *A Digest of Minnesota Election Laws*
(1967), *Financing Public Services in Minnesota* (1966), *Human
Resources: Minnesota's Changing Patterns* (1965), *Minnesota's
Twin Cities Metropolitan Area* (1966), *The State You're In*
(1958), *A Metropolitan Sanitary District in '67?* (1966), and
Indians in Minnesota (1962).

The League has advocated legislation for aid to dependent
children, for low-income housing, for improvement of public
health, for fair employment practices, for an increase in the
minimum school year, for consolidation of school districts, for
safeguards of teacher tenure and teacher retirement funds, and
for compulsory school attendance. Particularly interested in
structural and constitutional reforms, the Minnesota League has
been a constant and patient supporter of constitutional revision,
party designation for legislators, joint election of the governor
and lieutenant governor, legislative reapportionment, registration for lobbyists, election law recodification, and civil service.
Throughout its existence it has also campaigned for international

cooperation and for support of the League of Nations and the United Nations.

Organizationally the Minnesota League operates on local, state, and (as a member of the National League of Women Voters) national levels. Its members may meet, study, and "act" in small discussion units; they may also participate in local, area, and statewide annual assemblies and conventions. The governing power at the state and national levels resides in elective boards of directors who during their term of office are forbidden to engage in political party work. Local units must approve issues selected for study and for support. Use of study materials and handbooks and recourse to expert consultants are encouraged in all phases of the programming.

Preparatory to a legislative session the League may ask lawmakers where they stand on such issues as party designation and reapportionment. After the session opens the state office issues "Legislative Reports" giving committee appointments, times and places of committee meetings, and schedules of important hearings. League members are encouraged to attend and in some cases to testify; few are the days when members of the League cannot be seen attending committee hearings or "speaking to their representatives."

"Legislative Bulletins" and "Capitol Letters" provide additional information, as for example important committee votes not recorded in the press and testimony pertinent to League-supported issues. In "After Action" reports, measures in which the League is interested are traced from their introduction through all the stages of committee hearings, floor battles, and votes. These case histories explain successes and failures, single out the positive and negative contributions of legislators, analyze proponents' and opponents' speeches, and probe into parliamentary delaying tactics.

Cartoons and jokes about "women in politics" notwithstanding, no one can deny the sincere, intelligent, and professional approach of League workers. Supporters acclaim the perennial championing by the League of neglected, unspectacular, and vital issues involving technical and structural reforms. Whereas capitol corridors teem with people who want something for themselves at their neighbor's expense, the genius of the League lies in its disinterestedness and in the emphasis it puts on the basic questions of political philosophy.

The strengths of the League become its weaknesses when seen from another point of view. Its detractors read the prejudices of the well educated and the well-to-do into the League's activities and accuse it of failing in representativeness. Working girls might well be uncomfortable in a League study session where the atmosphere and vocabulary resemble those of a meeting of the American Association of University Women. Conservatives have looked askance at the League's fondness for fair employment practices, public housing, and related social welfare measures. In such quarters its preoccupation with constitutional revision and legislative reapportionment has been interpreted as an "egghead" tinkering with the status quo, and it has been associated in some minds with urban pressure groups or with labor union policies. Some candidates upon receiving League questionnaires before an election complain that such queries represent an invasion of their privacy and a threat to their independence — but such criticism may redound more to the candidate's discredit than the League's.

League friends and critics alike concede without much debate that League members are well informed and persevering, that their legislative spokesmen are highly competent, that they are not afraid to fight for what they consider right.

The Minnesota Association of Commerce and Industry

"The role of the Minnesota Employers Association [former name of the Minnesota Association of Commerce and Industry] in the area of state and federal legislation is to be a central source of information, indeed a clearinghouse for the multiple viewpoints expressed by various business firms and trade and professional organizations in the state. We will then be in a position to offer a coordinated program representing a level of agreement among business that tends to benefit all economic segments of the state." The preceding statement was excerpted from a statement of "principles, objectives and suggested policy positions" of this organization. Nationally affiliated with various other business and industrial councils, the Minnesota association comprises some 1,450 member companies. It was founded in 1908 to help create a favorable legislative climate for business. Membership is open to all employers of nine or more and dues are computed on the basis of fifty cents for every $1,000 of annual payroll subject to the state's unemployment compensation tax, but with a minimum of $25 and a maximum of $750.

The association has a 37-member Board of Directors which meets at least annually, but the responsibility for the real legislative work lies elsewhere. For many years Otto F. Christianson, the organization's executive vice-president, acted as its chief spokesman and lobbyist, delivering hundreds of speeches to civic, business, professional, and fraternal groups throughout the state. During the legislative sessions he testified before committees, supplied research materials that supported the case for employers and presented arguments in favor of economy and stability in government. More informally he sought to create legislative good will through luncheons and social occasions to which lawmakers were invited.

He was known on the Hill as an extremely well informed and tireless lobbyist. Fundamentally conservative, he vehemently opposed all those measures commonly associated with the welfare state, fought against constitutional revision and party designation, and condemned anything that might reinforce the power of organized labor. He kept a wary eye on governmental budgets and appropriations and was quick to expose what he considered unnecessary expenditures imposing new burdens on already hard-pressed taxpayers. To the Liberals he often appeared to be the very symbol of business reaction, blindly opposing the broadening base of social and economic power and resisting the claims of human values over profits and property.

After Mr. Christianson retired in June 1967, a great deal

of organizational restructuring took place. The association has changed from a tight, vertical structure to a broader, more horizontally organized group, which is concerned with broad participation and which seeks ties and cooperation with other business and trade associations for the attainment of a common end. The association was recently structured into five major divisions (Governmental Relations, Public Affairs, Employee Relations, Economic Development, and Internal Operations) and a large number of standing committees were created, with membership not limited to association members only. The association sees itself as taking on the color of a state chamber of commerce in the formation of its committees to deal with specific problems. This restructuring has been reflected in a basic shift in lobbying tactics and strategy. As the association sees it, the real task of lobbying is to provide facts and figures to the "new breed" of young, intelligent representatives who have come to the capitol from the state's urban and suburban areas as a result of reapportionment. The goal is to become recognized by these legislators as the source of authoritative information on areas of concern to both the association and the legislature.

Meanwhile, members are kept informed of events on the Hill by means of regular "Legislative Reports" (written by the association's vice-president and general manager, Oliver S. Perry, its director of public affairs, Ira B. Rogers, and its employee relations adviser, Harry D. Peterson) in the association's bulletin, *Guidepost,* and by articles appearing in *The Employer,* its monthly magazine. These reports list committee members, analyze bills affecting employers' interests, and discuss the tactics of the opposition forces. At the beginning of the 1959 session, for example, the board unanimously condemned the governor's budget message which "although proposing millions for relief and welfare . . . suggested nothing for increasing employment. . . . Apparently the Governor has thrown his lot with those who hold little hope for the future of business and industry in our state . . . such as encouraging business to come to or expand in Minnesota. In fact he offers industry ample incentive to expand elsewhere or to leave the state." Reports in subsequent issues of *The Guidepost* revealed the type of legislation opposed by the association: temporary disability insurance, upward revision of the unemployment compensation rates, and equal pay for equal work done by women. The association has supported the taconite amendment to the state constitution, "realistic" standards for control of air and water pollution, governmental reorganization for efficiency and economy, along with increase in legislative staff personnel and better physical facilities for the legislature.

Friends and enemies will agree that the Minnesota Association of Commerce and Industry (whether under this label or under its former name, the Minnesota Employers' Association) has given its clients their money's worth. "The MEA can look upon the 1953 session of the Minnesota legislature," political reporter Fred Neumeier wrote in the *St. Paul Pioneer Press* in May 1953, "as a success. Not one bill opposed by the association became law. The recommendations . . . on workmen's compensation and unemployment compensation were adopted. The association fought labor bosses to a standstill on their efforts to toss out state laws restricting the activities of unions." Though less successful in 1955 and 1957 in blocking this and other labor-supported laws, the association during the 1959 session assisted in defeating bills that would have increased workmen's and unemployment compensation benefits and would have broadened their coverage to include employees of charitable hospitals. An index of the association's strength might be found in a few statistics on some of the important measures it "watched" during the 1959 session. Of 53 labor measures introduced into the house (43 of which were Liberal-sponsored) all but two were killed either in that chamber or in the senate; of 26 unemployment compensation bills (24 of which had Liberal backing) only 4 survived; and of the 25 measures on workmen's compensation (the Liberals introduced 21), 20 failed. In the 1967 legislative session, the association was successful in obtaining the passage of no fewer than ten bills which it strongly supported, ranging from the sales tax and tax reform bill to a bill allowing local referendum on the sale of liquor on Sundays and reorganization of the Economic Development Department.

The Minnesota AFL-CIO Federation of Labor

Although some union activity goes back to the early 1830's, large-scale organization of American labor had to wait until the post-Civil War decades. Hard times in the 1870's accelerated unionization and brought on strikes. In Minnesota, the St. Paul Trades and Labor Assembly was founded in 1882, the Minneapolis Trades Assembly one year later, and the Minnesota State Federation of Labor in 1890. From the beginning the question of political activity by unions loomed large, and after a bitter battle among Socialists, Progressives, and others included in its membership, the Federation of Labor added a clause to its constitution in 1896 to the effect that "Party politics, whether they be Democratic, Republican, Socialist, Populistic, or Prohibition, or any other, shall have no place in the conventions of this Federation, nor shall the delegates of any political party be admitted."

Yet legislative issues, especially when conceived narrowly in terms of wages, hours, and living conditions, have involved the Federation of Labor throughout its existence with politics and politicians. Generally although by no means uniformly inclined toward the Farmer-Labor party and the DFL, the Minnesota State Federation has found it expedient to develop an effective working relationship with the long line of Republican governors and the Conservative leaders of the Minnesota legislature. There have even been instances of the Federation of Labor endorsing Republicans in congressional elections on the principle of "rewarding friends and punishing enemies."

An indication of the current political potential of organized labor in Minnesota is to be found in its sheer weight of numbers; since the AFL-CIO merger in 1956, the combined strength of organized labor (including the various railroad brotherhoods and other independent union movements) has been approximately 175,000 members.

In addition to its immediate concern with labor problems per se, the Minnesota labor movement has given past or present support to many general reforms, such as provision of free textbooks for school children, abolition of the convict contract system, strengthening of education on the elementary, secondary, vocational, and adult levels, state governmental reorganization, initiative, referendum, and recall, income taxation, veterans' benefits, party designation, constitutional revision, legislative reapportionment, state civil service, fair employment practices, and income tax withholding. Its overriding concern during the 1930's was of course the issue of relief and unemployment compensation for the jobless and hungry. Led by such men as E. G. Hall, Robert A. Olson, George A. Lawson (Federation of Labor secretary, 1914–54), Robert Hess, and David Roe, Minnesota labor has fought against anti-secondary-boycott laws, union suability, "right to work" laws, no-strike laws for public employees, and a general sales tax.

Structurally, the Federation of Labor is governed by its biennial conventions and its special conferences. Between conventions decisions on legislative questions are made by an executive committee headed by President Roe, Executive Vice-President Leonard Lashomb, and Secretary-Treasurer Neil C. Sherburne. This committee includes twenty-five other vice-presidents representing important union groupings. Committees on legal problems, research, public relations, and political education are responsible to the executive committee, which in turn is responsible to the 1,000-delegate convention, attended by representatives from 625 unions, 38 local departments (building, metals, etc.), and 26 city central bodies (trade and labor assemblies). Membership dues for the affiliated local unions are based on a per-capita tax of twelve cents per member per month. There is a fee of $1 per year per convention delegate from each city central body and $2 from each affiliated organization.

Much of the lobbying done by the Minnesota labor movement has been the work of the federation's executive leaders, such men as Robert Olson, David Roe, Robert Hess, Neil Sherburne, Frank Starkey, and William D. Gunn, and of the representatives of the various railroad brotherhoods, as for example Elmer Bergelund, the chairman and legislative representative of the Brotherhood of Railroad Trainmen. Research staffs provide background data on the thirty to fifty measures sponsored or supported by the labor movement in each session, and they offer help to friendly legislators in search of ammunition to counteract the lobbying efforts of business, taxpayer, and other groups hostile to labor objectives. Union publications keep tab on lawmakers and biennial legislative reports give each legislator's vote on selected issues of concern to labor, together with brief discussions of parliamentary successes, failures, and obstacles. Labor leaders have found this material useful in keeping campaigns centered on issues and in educating union members about the causes for which labor fights.

For either tactical or ideological reasons the Federation of Labor was for many years much more reluctant than the younger CIO to join forces with New Dealers and Fair Dealers; more recently Minnesota labor has cooperated more openly with other liberal groups, has broadened its interests to include more general social and humanitarian goals, and has sought rapprochement with certain state farm and cooperative organizations. Its influence within DFL councils and its effective support of friendly legislators have given the labor movement considerable legislative leverage. This was particularly true in the 1955 and 1957 sessions.

As with any other pressure group, an evaluation depends on one's own point of view. Critics evince considerable alarm at the burgeoning power of organized labor within the DFL and the Liberal caucus of the house. Conservative opposition to party designation, constitutional revision, and other Liberal-sponsored issues which labor supports may help to explain the old-guard position on the political activities of labor. For their part, labor leaders insist that their power has been grossly exaggerated. They complain of being used as whipping boys by conservative interests who seek to isolate them from their rank and file and who seek to isolate the labor movement as a whole from the farmers by exploiting charges of labor racketeering and bossism. The broad modern objectives of labor, union leaders assert, are coincident with rather than inimical to the general welfare. They say that they fight an uphill battle at best in a state where disproportionate representation has until only very recently prevented genuine majority rule and where the opposition enjoys a near-monopoly of the means of communication.

The Minnesota Farm Bureau Federation

Since its founding in 1919 the Minnesota Farm Bureau Federation has grown to include over 30,000 farm families. Affiliated with the American Farm Bureau Federation and its 1.7 million families, the Minnesota group is a "free, independent, non-governmental, voluntary organization of farm and ranch families . . . to achieve educational improvement, economic opportunity, and social advancement." It further defines itself as "local, national and international in . . . scope and influence, and non-partisan, non-sectarian, and non-secret in character." It claims to speak for all kinds of farmers and to be the true "Voice of Organized Agriculture," and it insists that the leaders and the voting members of the organization must be farmers.

The organizational philosophy of the Farm Bureau places sovereignty at the grass roots. The county is the basic unit of the organization, and policies are passed on to the state level only after receiving majority approval at the lower level. In state conventions voting strength is based on county membership, each county being allotted at least one vote plus additional votes where membership exceeds 600. State board members are elected at these annual conventions, as well as an executive board which carries out policies approved by convention resolutions. The headquarters staff includes an executive secretary-treasurer, a director of the field and health services department, five district field men, and additional staff personnel engaged in information, research, public relations, and legislative contacts.

The general position taken by the Minnesota Farm Bureau Federation can be gauged by listing some of the main themes of the resolutions ratified during its convention in November 1966. It went on record as being against increases in federal aid to education, in favor of an amendment to the federal Constitution allowing prayer in the public schools, in favor of retention of section 14(b) of the Taft-Hartley Act, in favor of an amendment to the federal Constitution allowing one house of state legislatures to apportion on some basis other than population; it recommended that all able-bodied relief recipients be employed; it disapproved of a state constitutional convention, asserting that the amendment process would permit necessary revisions; it strongly supported a general sales tax. It urged the publishing of the names of juvenile offenders to curb youthful crime. It recommended that the governor and lieutenant governor be elected on the same ticket, but remained opposed to party designation for state legislators. Expressing concern over "a growing disrespect for the law in this country," it urged local communities to support law-enforcement agencies and further urged "a re-examination of recent court rulings which have tended to place the rights of the criminal above the rights of the citizen against whom the crime has been committed."

The federation has also opposed income-tax-withholding plans and gasoline tax increases, but has urged that the personal property tax on all items, except for real estate currently classified as personal property, be repealed and that state-collected funds be returned to each local taxing district, dollar for dollar, to replace the lost revenue. In the area of education it has favored a greater emphasis on the "principles and philosophy of the American system of self-government and its accompanying private competitive enterprise system." It regards itself as the sponsor or steady friend of marketing and bargaining associations such as the Central Livestock Association, the Land O'

Lakes Cooperative Marketing Association, the Twin Cities Milk Producers Association, and the Midwest Wool Growers Marketing Association, and as a contributor to the beginnings of the Blue Cross–Blue Shield health insurance programs.

Geographically, Minnesota Farm Bureau strength is concentrated in the 1st and 2nd Congressional districts, which include Minnesota's "deep south" counties of Blue Earth, Mower, Jackson, Fillmore, Freeborn, Cottonwood, and Clay. Scott, Dakota, and McLeod counties, a little to the north, are also Farm Bureau bastions, as are parts of the 6th and 7th Congressional districts, in particular Polk, Kittson, Meeker, and Stearns counties.

Table 8. Minnesota Farm Bureau Strength Compared with Conservative-Liberal Representation in the Legislature (1967)

No. of Bureau Members per Legislative District	Conservatives	Liberals	Conservative Advantage	
			No.	%
900 and over	24	10	14	71
700–899	4	0	4	100
500–699	14	3	11	82
300–499	31	14	17	69
100–299	13	6	7	68

Table 8 shows a rather definite concurrence between Conservative representation in the legislature and Farm Bureau strength. Since many other factors are involved (as, for example, land values and the personalities of the individual candidates) it would be absurd to impute a cause-and-effect relationship to these figures; nevertheless the potent influence of the Farm Bureau Federation on the Minnesota legislature is beyond question.

What is involved here is something more than mere lobbying. Granted that the Farm Bureau provides legislators with research materials and keeps in year-round touch with them not only by mail but also by personal contact through its executive secretary-treasurer K. A. Snyder, its president P. D. Hempstead, and its legislative director Vern Ingvalson, it still seems likely that the organization's program succeeds chiefly because so many legislators are themselves farmers. If not actually tilling the soil, many of them are engaged in occupations so closely interwoven with farming (banking, real estate, small-town business, small-town legal practice, weekly newspapers) that their thinking and voting may be rather naturally in harmony with the thinking of the Farm Bureau leadership.

This raises again the question of how democratic and inclusive the organization in fact is. Its opponents suspect it of being led by and for the upper-income farmer, the corporation farmer, farm-connected industries, and even chambers of commerce. Some consider that despite its local foundations it is dominated by a bureaucracy that imposes its views or those of the national organization on the individual members. Organized labor has little cause for friendship with the Farm Bureau, which has always opposed what it considers to be monopoly union power and compulsory unionization, and has favored economy in government even at the expense of some welfare legislation. Proponents of political reforms (such as an overhaul and centralization of state administration, reapportionment, and reduction of the number of elective offices) feel that the conservative resistance of the federation has had much to do with their legislative defeats.

Spokesmen for the Farm Bureau counter these arguments with some of their own. Theirs is a farmers' organization, they explain, which opposes urban pressures and big government and socialism on principle, but is not supine or uncreative. The federation claims credit for better roads, for genuine farm cooperatives, for reducing marketing costs, for a brucellosis control program, for crop research, for sponsoring rural electrification, for playing a major role in what it maintains has been a much-needed and long-sought property tax relief and reform in Minnesota. Consistent with its own minimized-government doctrines, it has remained hostile to government aid for farmers whether through production payment plans, acreage reductions, or high and rigid price supports. In the federation's own words, "the future of farming depends on its being a free [and] competitive enterprise . . . regulated by supply and demand and with as few regulations as necessary."

The Minnesota Farmers Union

Unlike the rival Farm Bureau Federation, the Minnesota Farmers Union (in operation by 1930) has never been known for conservative inclinations. Strongly tied to the politics of protest, dissent, and Populism, the Farmers Union has been extremely critical of various aspects of capitalism, particularly of the profit and credit mechanism. Throughout its existence it has prided itself on speaking for the "little fellow" and the "real dirt farmer."

The base of its organizational pyramid is its claimed membership of over 25,000 families. Each chartered county union elects a president; these county presidents compose a state board of directors and elect from their members annually an executive committee of five members, one of whom serves as state president. Policies are formulated at the annual conventions in which each local unit wields voting strength in proportion to its membership.

"The family-type farm is the keystone of our policy," according to the preamble of a 1967 Farmers Union publication. In the interests of protecting and improving the status of the family farm the Farmers Union has not hesitated to call upon the state or federal government for action and intervention. It has approved of state income tax withholding, low-cost public power, and the establishment of a "rural electric and telephone loan bank," which should be "assisted with federal appropriations and private capital funds to provide loan funds needed by cooperative power and telephone systems." Its attitudes toward labor differ markedly from those of the Farm Bureau. "Farmers should recognize," the Farmers Union states, "that the so-called 'right to work' laws are not designed to protect the workers, but rather to undermine the system of collective bargaining which organized labor has developed over a period of years." Members are urged to do business with the Farmers Union

121

Central Exchange, the Farmers Union Grain Terminal Association, and Farmers Union Insurance.

The Farmers Union strongly opposed the state general retail sales tax which was passed in 1967 by the state legislature. It asks for tax relief for "farmers, small-business men and wage earners." Believing real estate and personal property taxes to be too high, the organization supports "tax proposals which would base personal property taxes on net income earned by the property, rather than book value of the property." It has a program of educational aims, including strengthening of the University of Minnesota branch system, federal aid for the construction of schools, and expanded aid for support of public schools. It urges adoption of the "Heller plan" for the return of federal income tax money to the states, favors an increase in social security benefits and an expansion of Medicare by the state legislature, taking full advantage of Title 19 of the Social Security Act of 1965, and recommends that "federal minimum wage laws should apply to migratory agricultural labor and to any persons employed in integrated farm operations." The Farmers Union wants party designation for legislators and annual legislative sessions, and opposes the seniority system in the assignment of legislative committee posts.

The community of interest between farmer and laborer has become a basic tenet of the Farmers Union. In bringing together organized labor and the cooperative movement it hopes to generate legislative power to convert its objectives (many of which are labor's as well) into laws, regulations, and state-sponsored services.

Representing the Minnesota Farmers Union at the legislature and working closely with M. W. Thatcher, the general manager of the Grain Terminal Association, are the organization's longtime president, Edwin Christianson, and the executive secretary, Archie Baumann. In its weekly newsletters and bimonthly newspapers the Farmers Union makes no secret of its generally strong support of the DFL and the Liberal caucus. Its party proclivities are also indicated by the numerous speaking ap-

Table 9. Comparison of Farmers Union Strength and Liberal-Conservative Representation in Legislature (1967)

No. of Farmers Union Member Families per Legislative District	Liberals	Conservatives	Conservative Advantage
900 and over	22	27	5
700 to 899	5	16	11
500 to 699	18	33	15

pearances made by Hubert Humphrey, Orville Freeman, Eugene McCarthy, Walter Mondale, and various DFL congressmen at conventions and banquets of the Farmers Union, the Grain Terminal Association, and the Central Exchange. In rural counties many of the DFL precinct workers are active in the farm and elevator cooperatives. Some interrelationship between degree of strength of the Minnesota Farmers Union and Conservative loss of power might be inferred from Table 9 — though here again multiple factors make it hazardous to assume a cause-and-effect relationship.

Whereas the Minnesota Farm Bureau is entrenched in the southern counties, Farmers Union strength comes from central and western Minnesota and from the Red River Valley in particular.

Being so unlike the Farm Bureau, the Farmers Union has drawn the opposite brand of criticism. To the conservative, its "government-consciousness" smacks of socialism. Its cooperation with organized labor arouses in some rural quarters an instinctive suspicion of unions and union bosses. The leftist tendencies of some extremist Farmers Union leaders back in the 1930's further aggravated these antagonisms. Today Farmers Union leaders, however, maintain that their organization is the one truly liberal force in agriculture, and that the family farm and the farmers' cooperative represent rural America's best bulwark against the ruthless and impersonal industrialization of modern agriculture.

The Minnesota Education Association

The Minnesota Education Association "makes no political commitments, recognizes no political alignments . . . and it seeks the good will and cooperation of all groups, confident that the education of the youth of Minnesota is a common interest — a common concern." As announced in its articles of incorporation, it proposes "to foster professional zeal, improve teaching, promote educational interests and advocate standards of education." Founded in 1861, it has a current membership of over 40,000 classroom teachers; principals, superintendents, and some faculty members from state and private colleges also belong.

Its more than 600 chartered and affiliated local chapters are grouped into Capital (St. Paul), Central, Hennepin (Minneapolis), Northeast, Northern, Southeast, Southwest, and Western divisions. They send delegates at the ratio of one for each 200 members to the 200-member annual assembly. Final authority lies in a 19-member board of directors which appoints an executive secretary to manage the day-to-day business at association headquarters: membership files, accounting, legislative contacts, field services, public relations, research, insurance, and publication of the *Minnesota Journal of Education* and *Minnesota Education News*. The association's executive secretary, A. L. Gallop, is one of the best known, most able, and most widely respected lobbyists on the Hill.

Like other interest groups the association considers it a major duty to inform its members about capitol affairs. Newsletters report on senate and house committee activities and discuss bills and proposals affecting school interests. The periodical *Windows on Legislation* is edited by Gallop. To supplement its normal legislative contacts, the association headquarters issues special "calls for help" to the membership during times of crisis; the result is a barrage of letters to a legislator or a committee chairman. Perhaps this device is one of the most effective weapons in the organization's arsenal.

As might be expected, the association's legislative program pertains chiefly though not exclusively to schools, teachers, and school finance. For years it has opposed the diversion of permanent school funds to any purpose other than primary and secondary education. Its "platform" has included among other things (1) increased state aid to school districts (up to 50 percent of the total cost of maintaining Minnesota's public elementary and secondary schools); (2) establishment of "a sound retirement program" for teachers; (3) passage of legislation "that would recognize the principle of limited liability" for school districts; (4) improvements of and additions to teacher placement services provided by the State Department of Education; (5) further school district consolidation and reorganization; (6) legislation to establish a professional practices board to protect the professional status of Minnesota's teachers and "to give the teaching profession the authority to protect the public from unethical conduct and unprofessional performance by teachers"; (7) salary increases for the faculties of state colleges; and (8) measures to make higher education facilities available to all youth in Minnesota.

The Minnesota Education Association has had considerable success in converting its objectives into state law. Among other things it has helped secure a state teacher tenure act, state aids to school districts amounting to 47 percent of support, a teachers' negotiation bill, and accelerated consolidation of school districts. All things considered, the association's capitol batting average is higher than that of most lobbies, partly because its well-educated, professionalized membership applies pressure on behalf of a cause to which the state, following frontier tradition, has already become deeply committed. Legislators who can turn a deaf ear to most blandishments are reluctant to "offend the teachers." Too, the organization has influential Conservative friends who will support appropriations for education despite their habitual unwillingness to spend money on "less worthy" enterprises.

Not everybody looks with unqualified favor on the Minnesota Education Association. It has working agreements with the Minnesota School Board Association and it has sometimes lobbied jointly with that group. Some teachers find it altogether too hospitable toward the school administrator's point of view and claim that they were pressured into joining by principals or superintendents who prefer this organization to the Minnesota Federation of Teachers. For these and other reasons, the federation detects a "company union" taint in the Minnesota Education Association and accuses it of reflecting "managerial interests" rather than the classroom teacher's.

Some of the other lobbies

To paraphrase Gilbert and Sullivan, a legislator's lot is not a happy one. These six lobbies and many more demand attention from the lawmaker not only throughout the 120-day session but intermittently during his full term as well.

Consider some of the other pressure groups competing for the legislator's support. The Minnesota Association for Mental Health has a coherent program backed by constant dissemination of facts and statistics. It claims that the state's excessive hospital readmission rates point to inadequate facilities, that psychiatric and other services are too heavily concentrated in the Twin Cities, that the state ought to finance increased research programs. The Minnesota Motor Transport Association, no weakling among lobbies, represents common carriers, petroleum carriers, livestock haulers, household goods movers, and almost everything else on rubber tires. It agitated through many sessions for the so-called fifty-foot truckers' bill — a measure opposed with equal vigor by the railroads and railroad brotherhoods. Add to these the Minnesota Taxpayers' Association, with its dedication to economy, its antagonism to income tax withholding, and its support of the sales tax. The Lake Superior Industrial Bureau is an organ through which the mining companies appeal for tax relief. Speaking through Phillip Hanft and Richard Hastings, it argues that increased costs and foreign competition will destroy Minnesota's great industry unless the legislature "gives them a break."

A familiar visitor to capitol corridors is Gordon Forbes, a former legislator who represents railroad interests. Two other ex-lawmakers, Lawrence Hall and Robert Dunlap, speak ably in behalf of the Wine and Spirits Institute and the Minnesota Brewers' Association respectively. Unlike them, the United Temperance Movement of Minnesota wants "to discourage the use of beverage alcohol and other narcotics . . . and . . . promote a higher standard of juvenile and adult conduct, prevent the disastrous effects of intemperance and kindred vices," and so on. While avoiding direct lobbying, the Minnesota Council of Churches alerts its membership to bills affecting social welfare, public morality, and education; and its member groups are quite apt to take pen in hand and relay their demands to their senate and house representatives.

Pleading causes, quoting figures, whitewashing themselves, indicting competitors, keeping government out, getting government in, urging expenditures, urging retrenchments, on they come along with the many other lobbies — a *vox populi* which is not always a *vox Dei.*

And yet it should be reiterated that the lobbies' "right to petition" is undeniable, as is their useful service in keeping hundreds of channels open between the lay person and the professional politician. If the lobbies have become an unofficial house of representatives, this is not necessarily an evil; lobby-less politics might be neater and simpler (though even this is hypothetical) but it would be far less interesting, and, more important, it would be far less representative.

Conflicts of interest

There is an inevitable overlapping between the membership or executive personnel of interest groups and the membership of the legislature. Some lobbies employ a former legislator as their representative, knowing that such a man's personal contacts and political experience will stand them in good stead. A lawyer-legislator may be retained by a particular client not so much because of his professional competence as because of his connections with "sources of power," and he may be paid an unexpectedly handsome fee for minor legal services. There is a great range of inducements — furtive or open, innocent or corrupt — to which legislators are subjected: luncheons, vacation trips, business favors, campaign contributions, and so on.

One can easily see the moral ambiguities here. In defense of the legislator it should be remembered that he is a part-time politician-statesman who is expected to keep his professional or business activities alive during his term of office. Perhaps inevitably he will represent some partial interest or interests which may at times conflict with the general interest, since he is himself elected from a geographical section, supported by a particular faction, and conditioned by his own experiences to a distinct point of view. It is extremely difficult, then, to define the point at which conflicts between special interests and the public interest lead to betrayals of the public trust. Though it can be asserted in a general sense that "no man can serve two masters" the application of this maxim to government is another matter.

In 1957 Governor Freeman appointed a bipartisan Committee on Ethics in Government which was first headed by President Charles J. Turck of Macalester College and later by Rabbi W. Gunther Plaut of St. Paul's Mount Zion Temple. The committee's report in 1958 drew widely from federal and state experiences (particularly in Wisconsin, New York, and California) and addressed itself to a host of related topics involving conflicts of interest, mandatory codes of ethics, campaign tactics, and lobbying. However, legislative implementation of its recommendations has been inconclusive to date. The 1959 session defeated a bill to create a governor's Commission on Ethical Standards together with a code of ethics for legislative as well as administrative personnel. The house overwhelmingly approved a bill (although this did not become law) requiring registration of lobbyists, disclosure of their objectives and activities, and financial accounting — all under criminal penalty for willfully disregarding the requirements or falsifying information. Disliking this approach, the senate adopted a rule (with the Liberals in near-unanimous opposition) requiring a lobbyist merely to register and to disclose to the committee before which he appears whether he "has a pecuniary or other special interest in a measure or proposal different from the public generally." Falsification while not bearing a criminal penalty would bar the offender from again "appearing" before the legislature in any "professional or representative capacity."

There is increasing demand for statutes to regulate legislative influence. Who should be exempted, who is technically a lobbyist and who is not, how frequent and how complete a financial reporting is to be required, who is to enforce what penalties — such are the considerations complicating legislation on the subject. The constitutionally sanctioned right of individuals and groups to speak, to earn a living and to enjoy reasonable financial privacy must be balanced against the right of the public to be represented by men whose ultimate allegiance is given to the total welfare rather than to a small fraction thereof.

Supplementary Materials

MINNESOTA'S DELEGATES TO THE NATION

A COMPLETE list of Minnesota's congressmen may be found in the 1965–66 *Legislative Manual*. The sketches here are intended to provide some biographical details on the senators who have served the state in the twentieth century and on a few of the more recent representatives from each of the congressional districts.

United States senators

Knute Nelson (1843–1923) was born in Norway but educated in the United States. A Civil War veteran, he moved to Minnesota from Wisconsin in 1871 and operated a farm near Alexandria. His public positions included attorney for Douglas County, state senator, and governor (1893–95). He was a Republican. In the United States Senate from 1895 to 1923 he supported the hard-money position against the inflationary demands of the Populists and Silver Republicans, and along with many other midwestern senators worked for downward revision of tariffs.

Moses Clapp (1851–1929) also moved to the state from Wisconsin. He became a Fergus Falls criminal lawyer and Minnesota attorney general. In 1901 as a regular Republican he was elected over the Silver Republican Charles A. Towne to the Senate vacancy created by the death of Cushman K. Davis. Clapp, known as "the Black Eagle," became the Senate expert on the problems of the Chippewa Indians and on Indian reservations; for a number of years he chaired the Senate Committee on Indian affairs. He also fought for the Hepburn and Elkin acts aimed at regulation of discriminatory rate and rebate practices of the railroads. His Senate incumbency lasted until 1917.

New York-born Frank B. Kellogg (1856–1937) came with his parents to Minnesota at the age of nine. As a St. Paul attorney he became an authority on corporation law. He served on the Interstate Commerce Commission and participated in the Standard Oil and Harriman railroad trust investigations. A Republican, he was elected to the Senate in 1916. As a member of its Foreign Relations Committee, he was one of those who had "mild reservations" about the League of Nations. In 1921–22 he represented the Senate majority party in the Washington arms conferences. Defeated by Henrik Shipstead in 1922, he became United States ambassador to Britain during the Harding administration, in which capacity he took part in the "Dawes plan" negotiations over German war debts. Calvin Coolidge appointed him secretary of state in 1925. He will be remembered for important policy decisions regarding Chinese-American relations and especially for the Kellogg-Briand "outlawry of war" pact signed on August 27, 1928. One year later he received the Nobel peace prize.

Henrik Shipstead (1881–1960), Kellogg's successful Senate opponent, was born in Burbank, Kandiyohi County, practiced dentistry in Glenwood, was that town's mayor from 1911 to 1913, and served as state representative from 1916 to 1921. After breaking off his association with the Republican party, he became the new Farmer-Labor party's first United States senator in 1923. He returned to the Republican fold in 1940. After serving four terms, he was defeated by Edward J. Thye in the 1946 Republican primary.

The highly colorful Magnus Johnson (1871–1936) emigrated from Sweden, worked as a lumberjack in northern Minnesota, Wisconsin, and Michigan, and settled on a 40-acre Meeker County farm in 1893. After terms in the state house of representatives (1915–19) and senate (1919–23) he gravitated toward the Farmer-Labor movement and was a member of the new party's founding committee. He became the Farmer-Laborites' second United States senator by reason of his 1923 victory in a special election for the seat of the deceased Knute Nelson. He was defeated the following year by Republican Thomas D. Schall, by a margin of 8,000 votes out of the 760,000 votes cast. He served one term in the United States House (1933–35), but was defeated in his bid for re-election.

Thomas D. Schall (1876–1935), born near Grand Rapids, Michigan, began his career as a newsboy and circus roustabout. Graduating from Hamline University and the St. Paul College of Law, he practiced law in Minneapolis until he lost his sight in 1907, the victim of a cigar-lighter explosion. He ran unsuccessfully for Congress on the Bull Moose ticket in 1912, but held the 10th District seat in the United States House of Representatives from 1915 to 1925. After his close senatorial victory over Magnus Johnson in 1924, it was charged that he had extorted money from bootleggers by promising them immunity from state or federal prosecution, but he was exonerated by state and senatorial investigating committees. In the Senate he was an implacable critic of the New Deal and of the Olson administration. He died in 1935 after an automobile accident. Governor Olson, who had himself intended to run against Schall in 1936, appointed Elmer Benson to the unexpired term.

Ernest Lundeen (1878–1940), a South Dakotan by birth and a Spanish-American War veteran, graduated from Carleton College and the University of Minnesota Law School. He was a Republican member of the Minnesota house for two terms starting in 1911, and in 1916 he won a seat in the famous War Congress of 1917–19, representing the 5th District. As an opponent of the Wilson administration, of conscription, and of American entry into the war, he was called by Teddy Roosevelt a "microbe" and "a shadow Hun." He became a Farmer-Laborite in the 1920's. He was elected at large to serve in the House of Representatives for the term 1933–35; he represented the 3rd District in Congress from 1935 to 1937. In 1936 he defeated former Governor Theodore Christianson by over 260,000 votes for the Senate, his stand on foreign affairs being an important issue in the campaign. He will be remembered chiefly for his unswerving isolationism but also for his strong support of New Deal social security measures (the Frazier-Lundeen Act). On August 31, 1940, he was killed in an airplane crash.

Joseph H. Ball (1905–   ) was born in Crookston, Minnesota. An alumnus of Antioch College and the University of Minnesota, he became a reporter on the *Minneapolis Journal* and later on the St. Paul newspapers, where he was an influential and widely read advocate of Stassen Republicanism. Governor Stassen named him to complete Senator Lundeen's term, a post he retained in the next election. A strong internationalist and independent, Ball deserted the Republicans briefly in 1944 to support Roosevelt's fourth term. The conservative labor position he adopted in supporting the Taft-Hartley bill became a salient issue in his 1948 contest with Democrat-Farmer-Laborite Hubert H. Humphrey, who defeated him.

Hubert H. Humphrey (1911–   ) was born in Wallace, South Dakota, graduated from the Denver College of Pharmacy, and was employed as a pharmacist from 1933 to 1937. He received his Bachelor of Arts degree from the University of Minnesota in 1939, his Master of Arts degree from the University of Louisiana in 1940. He served as state director of war production training and reemployment in 1941; state chief of the Minnesota War Service Program in 1942; assistant commissioner of the War Manpower Commission in 1943; instructor in political science at Macalester College, in St. Paul, 1943–44; mayor of Minneapolis, 1945–48. When elected to the upper house of Congress in 1948 he was the first DFL senator from the state. He was re-elected in 1954 and 1960. He served as Senate majority whip during his last term and was instrumental in the passage of such major legislation as the Civil Rights Act of 1964, the Nuclear Test Ban Treaty, the Food for Peace Program, and the Peace Corps, to mention just a few of his legislative efforts. Running with Lyndon B. Johnson, he was elected vice-president of the United States in 1964. In 1968 he won the Democratic presidential nomination — the first Minnesotan to head a national party ticket — but was defeated in the general election by Richard M. Nixon.

Of Norwegian parentage, Edward J. Thye (1896–1969) had been a Dakota County farmer since the early 1920's when he was appointed by Stassen as deputy commissioner of agriculture in 1939. Elected to the lieutenant governorship in 1942, Thye became the state's chief executive after Stassen departed for service in the Navy. In 1944 his popular mandate totaled 61.6 percent of the vote — the largest margin in any gubernatorial contest to date in the history of the state. Elected to the Senate in 1946 and re-elected in 1952 by a majority of 195,000 votes, Thye became a strong Eisenhower supporter on domestic and foreign policy issues and served on the Agriculture, Small Business, and Appropriations committees. He sponsored the Small Business Act, co-authored Public Law 480 and the Soil Bank plan, and supported the Farm Home Administration. He was defeated by Eugene J. McCarthy in 1958.

Eugene J. McCarthy (1916–) was born in Watkins, Minnesota, graduated from St. John's University in Collegeville, Minnesota, and took his M.A. degree at the University of Minnesota in 1939. He taught in public high schools and became a sociology instructor at the College of St. Thomas. He served as chairman of the Ramsey County DFL in 1948, and in November was elected to the United States House of Representatives. There he served on the House committees on Post Office and Civil Service, Agriculture, Interior and Insular Affairs, Banking and Currency, and Ways and Means (this last being the committee on committees for the House Democrats). He represented the Congress in various international meetings: the London Interparliamentary Conference in 1956, the Geneva Trade and Tariffs Conference in 1957, NATO parliamentary conferences in 1956 and 1957, and the World Health Conference in 1958. In the Senate McCarthy has been a member of the Finance, Foreign Relations, and Government Operations committees. The Americans for Democratic Action (ADA) rated him in the high 80's on its 100 percent scale for the 89th Congress. In the spring of 1968 McCarthy translated his criticism of the Johnson Vietnam policy into a vigorous campaign for the Democratic nomination for the presidency of the United States but lost out to Humphrey.

Walter F. Mondale (1928–) was born in Ceylon, Minnesota. He attended Macalester College, and graduated from the University of Minnesota with a B.A. in political science. He received his L.L.B degree from the University of Minnesota Law School in 1956, serving as a member of the Editorial Board of the *Law Review*. He was appointed attorney general of Minnesota in May 1960, winning election to that post in November 1960 and re-election in 1962. He was appointed to fill the Senate seat of Vice-President-elect Hubert H. Humphrey in December 1964 and was elected to a full Senate term in 1966. He serves as a member of the Senate Banking and Currency Committee, the Committee on Agriculture and Forestry, and the Committee on Aeronautical and Space Sciences. Senator Mondale has concentrated much of his effort in the areas of consumer protection and foreign aid; he was the author of a "fair warning" amendment to the National Traffic and Motor Safety Act, the World Hunger bill of 1965, and the Clean Meat bill of 1968. He has also been active in drafting civil rights legislation, playing an important role in the passage of the Civil Rights Act of 1968. His legislative record during the 89th Congress earned him a score in the middle 90's from the ADA.

United States representatives

Minnesota was divided into nine congressional districts until the reapportionment of 1961, when the state lost a district. The 1961 reapportionment is shown in Figure 5. The Minnesota delegation elected in 1968 to the House of Representatives consisted of five Republicans and three DFLers. The Republicans are by and large middle-of-the-roaders on domestic policy and advocates of active participation in international affairs. The three DFL congressmen are all liberals, scoring consistently high on the ADA rating scale.

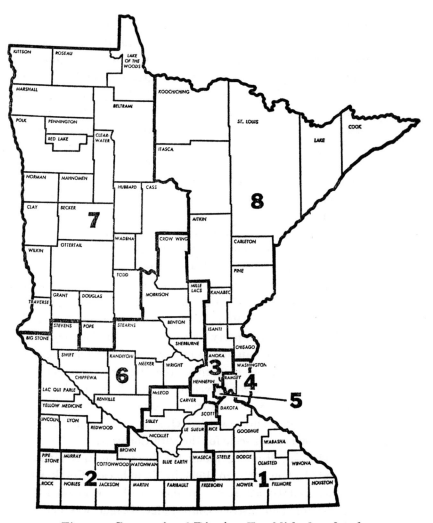

Figure 5. Congressional Districts Established under the
Reapportionment Act of 1961

1st District. This agriculturally rich southeastern sector, traditionally the center of Minnesota Republicanism, was for many years served by lawyer-farmer August H. Andresen of Red Wing, who was first elected from this district in 1934 (he represented the 3rd District from 1924 to 1935) and became ranking member of the House Agriculture Committee. Before World War II Andresen belonged to that group of midwestern congressmen who were extremely critical of any measures which would compromise American neutrality by involving this country in international or inter-Allied commitments. Though pro-Eisenhower, Andresen took issue with the president and the secretary of agriculture on a number of specific issues dealing with agriculture and the dairy industry.

When Andresen died, Albert H. Quie, who had served in two sessions of the state senate (1955 and 1957), narrowly won the seat at a special election in February 1958 against DFL contender Eugene Foley. Re-elected with large margins in 1958, 1960, 1962, 1964, 1966, and 1968, Quie serves on the House Committee on Education and Labor and the House Committee on Administration. He is a graduate of St. Olaf College, Northfield, Minnesota. In 1967 he co-authored "Opportunity Crusade," the Republican party's alternative to the War on Poverty. Quie has also taken an active interest in educational legislation, playing a major role in shaping the Higher Education Act of 1964 and the Manpower Development and Training Act of 1963. The Americans for Constitutional Action (ACA), a conservatively inclined group, awarded Quie a ranking in the middle 70's on a 100 percent scale for the 89th Congress.

2nd District. Running along the Iowa line, this region was represented from 1921 to 1933 by Republican Frank Clague, a former county attorney, speaker of the Minnesota house, state senator, and district court judge. Clague was one of the candidates for speaker of the United States House in 1931. Elmer J. Ryan was for a number of years the only Minnesota Democrat in Congress; he served from 1935 to 1941. Former McLeod County Attorney Joseph P. O'Hara represented the

2nd District from 1941 until his retirement in 1958. A perennial opponent of "big government," O'Hara objected to heavy expenditures for foreign aid, public power, and nationally administered or initiated welfare programs; he voted against giving the chief executive broad discretion in international commitments. Ancher Nelsen won the seat vacated by O'Hara in 1958. He has been re-elected continuously since 1960. He had served McLeod County in the state senate from 1935 to 1948, became lieutenant governor in 1953, and accepted an Eisenhower appointment to head the Rural Electrification Administration from 1953 to 1956. He was state Republican chairman from March to June 1958. Nelsen, who operates a 280-acre diversified farm in McLeod County, has shown particular interest in agricultural problems, in conservation programs, and in low-cost power for farmers. He serves on the House District of Columbia Committee (ranking minority member) and the Committee on Interstate and Foreign Commerce. The ADA gave him a score of 0 while the ACA assessed his record at 89 percent on its scale.

3rd District. This district, until 1961, covered northeast Minneapolis, rural Hennepin County, and several counties north and east of Minneapolis. The history of this district includes the 22-year congressional career of Charles R. Davis, a Republican who joined the Progressives' fight against the arbitrary rule of Speaker Cannon. His tenure ended in 1925. The 3rd District delegation since his time has included men of varied political backgrounds and viewpoints. Like his predecessor, Ernest Lundeen, Henry G. Teigan (1937–39) was prominently involved in early Farmer-Labor activities; he was editor of the Farmer-Labor *Advocate* and later of the *Minnesota Leader.* George MacKinnon, a devoted Stassen supporter in the state house of representatives from 1935 to 1941, represented the district in Congress from 1947 to 1949, during which time he voted in favor of such controversial measures as the Taft-Hartley labor bill, flexible price supports, and the Mundt-Nixon internal security bill. In the 1952 campaign MacKinnon acted as consultant to Nixon and in 1958, after service as United

States district attorney in Minnesota, he became the GOP candidate in the gubernatorial race against Orville Freeman. Roy W. Wier defeated MacKinnon in 1948 and was re-elected from that time to 1960, often by narrow margins. Before election to the congressional post, Wier served on the Minneapolis Board of Education (1939–49); he had been for 25 years the financial secretary and organizer of the Minneapolis Central Labor Union; and as state representative he had been a pro-Olson member of the Liberal caucus in the Minnesota legislature (1933–39). As a member of the United States House Education, Labor, and District of Columbia committees, he was a staunch supporter of Truman's Fair Deal program.

Since the reapportionment of 1961, the 3rd District has consisted of Anoka County and the part of Hennepin County outside of the city of Minneapolis, an area which includes that city's suburbs. Clark MacGregor was elected from the new district in 1960 and was re-elected in 1962, 1964, 1966, and 1968 by substantial margins. MacGregor is a graduate of Dartmouth College and the University of Minnesota Law School. He is a member of the House Committee on the Judiciary and was a member of the Select Committee on Adam Clayton Powell in 1967. As a member of the Judiciary Committee, MacGregor has taken an active interest in legislation promoting federal-state cooperation in law enforcement and federal aid to state law-enforcement agencies. He also played an active role in the passage of the Civil Rights Act of 1966, sponsoring (unsuccessfully) several amendments which would have strengthened the fair-housing section of that act. For the 89th Congress the ACA rated MacGregor at 74.

4th District. Except for one term in the mid-thirties, the 4th District (formerly St. Paul–Ramsey County; since 1961, it has included Washington County as well) was represented by Melvin J. Maas (Rep.) continuously from 1927 to 1945. Rather conservative on domestic issues, Maas was prominent in military and defense affairs, chaired the House Naval Affairs Committee, and alone among Minnesota congressmen voted for the fortification of Guam in 1939. A former marine combat officer who had lost his eyesight, Major General Maas served as chairman of the President's Committee on Employment of the Physically Handicapped. Succeeding him were Frank T. Starkey (DFL; 1945–47), St. Paul labor leader and later state commissioner of employment security under Governors Freeman and Rolvaag; Edward J. Devitt (Rep.; 1947–49), later United States district judge; and Eugene J. McCarthy (DFL; 1949–59), later United States senator. Joseph E. Karth (DFL) defeated Republican Frank S. Farrell by over 16,000 votes for the seat vacated by McCarthy. A World War II combat veteran, union official, and a four-term member of the Minnesota house (1951–59) and chairman of its Labor Committee, Karth serves on the Committee on Science and Astronautics and the Committee on Merchant Marine and Fisheries of the United States House of Representatives. He won re-election in 1960, 1962, 1964, 1966, and 1968. He has been a consistent supporter of Great Society legislation and has taken a special interest in the nation's space program (he chairs the Subcommittee on Space Sciences and Applications of the Committee on Science and Astronautics), particularly the Centaur and Surveyor programs. For the 89th Congress, the ADA rated him at 73.

5th District. This district, which now consists of the city of Minneapolis, has in recent decades sent a number of distinguished men to the House of Representatives. The list includes Walter H. Newton (Rep.; 1919–29), future secretary to President Hoover; W. I. Nolan (Rep.; 1929–33), a speaker of the Minnesota house and Minnesota's lieutenant governor from 1925 to 1929; Theodore Christianson (Rep.; 1935–37), three-term governor of Minnesota; and Dr. Walter H. Judd (Rep.; 1943–63). A native of Nebraska and a World War I veteran, Judd served for a number of years in South China as a medical missionary under the Foreign Mission Board of the Congregational church. As a highly influential member of the House Foreign Affairs Committee he became nationally known as a strong supporter of Chiang Kai-shek and the Nationalist China regime on Formosa. Among the many bills authored or sponsored by Judd were those dealing with United States membership in the United Nations and such related organizations as the World Health Organization, the International Children's Emergency Fund, and Technical Aid. He was a delegate to the United Nations General Assembly in 1957 and to the World Health assemblies in 1950 and 1958. In 1960 he was the keynote speaker at the Republican National Convention. Judd was defeated for re-election in 1962 by Donald M. Fraser. Fraser, son of Dean-emeritus Everett Fraser of the University of Minnesota Law School, is an attorney and former state senator (1955–63). He served in 1960 as chairman of Minnesota Citizens for Kennedy-Johnson and is secretary and whip of the Democratic Study Group, the "liberal caucus" of the House Democrats. A member of the House Foreign Affairs Committee, Fraser has been concerned with strengthening the role of the United Nations and is one of six congressional advisers to the Geneva disarmament conference. As a member of the District of Columbia Committee he has been interested in obtaining an elected school board and governmental reorganization and modernization for the District. Fraser belongs to Members of Congress for Peace through Law, and he has sponsored legislation calling for improved peacekeeping arrangements under the United Nations. He was a critic of the Johnson administration's Vietnam policy, although he supported Hubert Humphrey for the Democratic presidential nomination. During the 89th Congress he was rated at 100 by the ADA and at 0 by the ACA.

6th District. This district is the geographical center of Minnesota — an area that includes Stearns County and St. Cloud and shows a heavy concentration of voters of German descent. It was once represented by Charles A. Lindbergh (Rep.; 1907–17), who voted against United States entry into World War I and the Payne-Aldrich tariff, supported the Pujo investigations of the money trusts, and sided with the bloc of Republican insurgents and reformers. His congressional attacks on war profiteers and war propaganda furnished his opponents with lively campaign issues when he vied unsuccessfully with Burnquist for the gubernatorial nomination in the 1918 Republican primary. Harold Knutson, the Republican farmer-newspaper editor who represented the district from 1917 to 1933 and again from 1935 to 1949, rose to the chairmanship of the powerful House Ways and Means Committee. As one of the stalwarts of midwestern isolationism in the pre-Pearl Harbor era he opposed vigorously the New Deal, in both domestic and foreign policy. Fred Marshall (DFL; 1949–63) defeated Knutson in a close election in 1948 and during his seven terms in the House was the most direct and personal spokesman for agricultural interests among the DFL congressmen. Besides operating a fourth-generation family farm, Marshall served in the state Agricultural Adjustment Administration from 1937 to 1941 and held the office of state farm security administrator for seven years. Marshall declined to run for an eighth term and was succeeded by Alec G. Olson, who was elected in 1962 and again in 1964. Olson was a liberal with consistently high ratings from the ADA, and he was a consistent administration supporter. John Zwach (Rep.) of Walnut Grove defeated Olson in 1966. Zwach served for ten years (1935–45) in the Minnesota house of representatives and for twenty years (1947–67) in the state senate. He was for a long time the Conservative majority leader in the latter body. He is a member of the House Agriculture and House District of Columbia committees, and as such is interested, among other things, in legislation to regulate agricultural imports and to confer congressional representation upon the District of Columbia.

The Old 7th District. Until the reapportionment of 1961, the 7th District consisted of the southwestern area of the state along the South Dakota border (now largely included in the 2nd and 6th districts). It sent to Washington the famous Andrew J. Volstead (Rep.; 1903–23), the "father of prohibition." Volstead was a St. Olaf College graduate, city attorney and mayor of Granite Falls, and Yellow Medicine's county attorney; in the House he became chairman of the Judiciary Committee and was an important legislative figure in matters of federal law enforcement. O. J. Kvale (1923–29), a Lutheran minister and one of the few Farmer-Labor congressmen, defeated Volstead and served as spokesman for agricultural discontent until his accidental death. His son, Paul John Kvale, also a Farmer-Laborite, succeeded him but was defeated by H. Carl Andersen in 1938. A Republican and a Tyler, Minnesota, farmer, Andersen gave strong support to soil and water conservation programs. He also showed much interest in increased federal appropriations for cancer and heart research. On domestic issues Andersen generally sided with those midwestern Republicans who criticized the extension of international commitments and who resisted New and Fair Deal legislative objectives. In the 83rd Congress he was ranking minority member of the House Appropriations Committee.

7th District. This district, in Minnesota's sparsely populated northwestern corner, encompasses the area previously (before 1961) included in the 9th Congressional District. For many years it was second only to the present 8th Congressional District in its allegiance to the Farmer-Laborites. Farmer-Labor stalwart Knud Wefald represented the district from 1923 to 1927 and Richard Thompson Buckler from 1935 to 1943. Buckler, who had been the state senator from Polk County for twelve years, considered himself a follower of the true progressive tradition. In Congress he fought for farm cooperatives, for lower interest rates for farmers, for federal old-age pensions, and for governmental ownership and control of a central banking system. His successor, Harold C. Hagen (1943–55), once a Farmer-Laborite, later a Republican, had been a social studies teacher, an athletic coach, a newspaper publisher, and for eight years Buckler's congressional secretary. Besides speaking for agricultural interests Hagen showed much interest in the problems of postal employees and civil servants. In 1954 he was defeated by Mrs. Coya Knutson, a former music teacher and a two-term member of the legislature (1951 and 1953). In Congress she became the first woman member of the House Agricultural Committee and was identified with those new Democrats from the Midwest who opposed the Eisenhower position on agriculture, public power, credit, and taxation. During Mrs. Knutson's re-election bid in 1958 her husband's alleged objections to her political career grew into a nationally publicized "Coya Come Home" incident. She was defeated by Republican Odin Langen, a former state representative (1951–59) and minority leader in the Minnesota house during 1957. Langen has been re-elected continuously since 1960 and is generally known to be a conservative, scoring high (89) on the ACA scale. He is a member of the House Appropriations Committee and chairs the important House Minority Task Force on Agriculture.

8th District. Including Duluth, St. Louis County, and the iron-mining country, the 8th District is now a DFL stronghold, but it was earlier represented for fourteen years by Republican William A. Pittenger (1929–33, 1935–37, 1939–47). Pittenger graduated from Wabash College and the Harvard Law School, served in the state legislature (1917–19), and while in Congress made his influence felt in the Rivers and Harbors Committee, where he was an advocate of the St. Lawrence Seaway. He voted for the lend-lease agreements on the eve of World War II and for extension of the draft in 1941. Certain New Deal measures, as for example WPA and NYA, met with his approval. John A. Blatnik defeated Pittenger in 1946 and has been re-elected with huge majorities ever since; his 70,000 pluralities of 1956 and 1964 and his unopposed victory in 1966 standing as the most decisive victories in the history of the state's congressional elections. After graduating from Winona State Teachers College, Blatnik did postgraduate work in public administration at the universities of Chicago and Minnesota, taught school, and served in the state senate (1941), where he was instrumental in the passage of the Minnesota Taconite Tax Law. During World War II he served in Air Corps Intelligence and in the OSS and was a paratroop officer working behind enemy lines in northern Yugoslavia. As the dean of the DFL congressional delegation his major interests are natural resources, social welfare legislation, the St. Lawrence Seaway, federal water-pollution control, refugee and immigration measures, foreign aid, and support of the United Nations and its technical assistance programs. He is second-ranking majority member of the House Committee on Public Works (where he chairs the Subcommittee on Rivers and Harbors) and is also a member of the Committee on Government Operations. The ADA rated him at 89 for the 89th Congress.

GOVERNORS OF THE STATE

Name and Party	Term in Office
Territorial	
Alexander Ramsey	1849–1853
Willis A. Gorman	1853–1857
Samuel Medary	1857–1858
State	
Henry H. Sibley (Democrat)	1858–1860
Alexander Ramsey (Republican)	1860–1863
Henry A. Swift (Republican)	1863–1864
Stephen Miller (Republican)	1864–1866
William R. Marshall (Republican)	1866–1870
Horace Austin (Republican)	1870–1874
Cushman K. Davis (Republican)	1874–1876
John S. Pillsbury (Republican)	1876–1882
Lucius F. Hubbard (Republican)	1882–1887
Andrew R. McGill (Republican)	1887–1889
William R. Merriam (Republican)	1889–1893
Knute Nelson (Republican)	1893–1895
David M. Clough (Republican)	1895–1899
John Lind (Democrat)	1899–1901
Samuel R. Van Sant (Republican)	1901–1905
John A. Johnson (Democrat)	1905–1909
Adolph O. Eberhart (Republican)	1909–1915
Winfield S. Hammond (Democrat)	1915
Joseph A. A. Burnquist (Republican)	1915–1921
J. A. O. Preus (Republican)	1921–1925
Theodore Christianson (Republican)	1925–1931
Floyd B. Olson (Farmer-Labor)	1931–1936
Hjalmar Petersen (Farmer-Labor)	1936–1937
Elmer A. Benson (Farmer-Labor)	1937–1939
Harold E. Stassen (Republican)	1939–1943
Edward J. Thye (Republican)	1943–1947
Luther W. Youngdahl (Republican)	1947–1951
C. Elmer Anderson (Republican)	1951–1955
Orville L. Freeman (Democrat-Farmer-Laborite)	1955–1961
Elmer L. Andersen (Republican)	1961–1963
Karl F. Rolvaag (Democrat-Farmer-Laborite)	1963–1967
Harold LeVander (Republican)	1967–

VOTING STATISTICS

Table I. Major Party Vote for President in Minnesota, 1920–1968 [a]

Year	Candidate and Party	Votes Cast	Percentage of Total
1920	*Warren G. Harding* (Rep.)	519,421	70.6
	James M. Cox (Dem.)	142,994	19.4
	Eugene V. Debs (Soc.)	56,106	7.6
1924	*Calvin Coolidge* (Rep.)	420,759	51.2
	John W. Davis (Dem.)	55,913	6.8
	Robert M. LaFollette (Ind.)	339,192	41.3
1928	*Herbert Hoover* (Rep.)	560,977	57.8
	Alfred E. Smith (Dem.)	396,451	40.8
1932	*Franklin D. Roosevelt* (Dem.)	600,806	59.9
	Herbert Hoover (Rep.)	363,959	36.3
1936	*Franklin D. Roosevelt* (Dem.)	698,811	61.8
	Alfred M. Landon (Rep.)	350,461	31.0
1940	*Franklin D. Roosevelt* (Dem.)	644,196	51.5
	Wendell L. Willkie (Rep.)	596,274	47.7
1944	*Franklin D. Roosevelt* (Dem.)	589,864	52.4
	Thomas E. Dewey (Rep.)	527,416	46.9
1948	*Harry S. Truman* (Dem.)	692,966	57.2
	Thomas E. Dewey (Rep.)	483,617	39.9
1952	*Dwight D. Eisenhower* (Rep.)	763,211	55.3
	Adlai E. Stevenson (Dem.)	608,458	44.1
1956	*Dwight D. Eisenhower* (Rep.)	719,302	53.7
	Adlai E. Stevenson (Dem.)	617,525	46.1
1960	*John F. Kennedy* (Dem.)	779,933	50.6
	Richard M. Nixon (Rep.)	757,915	44.5
1964	*Lyndon B. Johnson* (Dem.)	991,417	63.7
	Barry M. Goldwater (Rep.)	559,624	36.0
1968	Hubert H. Humphrey (Dem.)	857,738	54.0
	Richard M. Nixon (Rep.)	658,643	41.5

[a] Votes for candidates of the Industrial Government party, Communist party, Socialist Worker party, and other minor political groups were omitted because of their small number of votes; hence the figures do not total 100 percent.

Table II. Major Party Vote for Senator in Minnesota, 1916-1966 [a]

Year	Candidate and Party	Votes Cast	Percentage of Total
1916	*Frank B. Kellogg* (Rep.)	185,159	48.6
	Daniel W. Lawler (Dem.)	117,541	30.8
	W. G. Calderwood (Prohib.)	78,425	20.6
1918	*Knute Nelson* (Rep.)	206,684	60.1
	W. G. Calderwood (Prohib.)	137,296	39.9
1922	*Henrik Shipstead* (FL)	325,372	47.1
	Frank B. Kellogg (Rep.)	241,833	35.0
	A. Olesen (Dem.)	123,624	17.9
1924	*Thomas D. Schall* (Rep.)	388,594	46.5
	Magnus Johnson (FL)	380,646	45.5
	John J. Farrell (Dem.)	53,709	6.4
1928	*Henrik Shipstead* (FL)	665,169	65.4
	Arthur E. Nelson (Rep.)	342,992	33.7
1930	*Thomas D. Schall* (Rep.)	293,626	37.6
	Ernest Lundeen (FL)	178,671	22.9
	Einar Hoidale (Dem.)	282,018	36.1
	Charles Lund (Ind. by Pet.)	20,669	2.6
1934	*Henrik Shipstead* (FL)	503,379	49.9
	H. J. Holmberg (Rep.)	200,083	19.8
	Einar Hoidale (Dem.)	294,757	29.2
1936	*Ernest Lundeen* (FL)	663,363	62.2
	Theodore Christianson (Rep.)	402,404	37.8
1940	*Henrik Shipstead* (Rep.)	641,049	53.0
	Elmer A. Benson (FL)	310,875	25.7
	John E. Regan (Dem.)	248,658	20.6
1942	*Joseph H. Ball* (Rep.)	356,297	47.0
	Elmer A. Benson (FL)	213,965	28.2
	Ed Murphy (Dem.)	78,959	10.4
	Martin A. Nelson (Ind. Prog.)	109,226	14.4
1946	*Edward J. Thye* (Rep.)	517,775	58.9
	Theodore Jorgenson (DFL)	349,520	39.8
1948	*Hubert H. Humphrey* (DFL)	729,494	59.8
	Joseph H. Ball (Rep.)	485,801	39.8
1952	*Edward J. Thye* (Rep.)	785,649	56.6
	William Carlson (DFL)	590,011	42.5
1954	*Hubert H. Humphrey* (DFL)	642,193	56.4
	Val Bjornson (Rep.)	479,619	42.1
1958	*Eugene J. McCarthy* (DFL)	608,847	52.9
	Edward J. Thye (Rep.)	535,629	46.6

[a] Votes for candidates of the Industrial Government party, Communist party, Socialist Worker party, and other minor political groups were omitted because of their small number of votes; hence the figures do not total 100 percent.

Table II — Continued

Year	Candidate and Party	Votes Cast	Percentage of Total
1960	*Hubert H. Humphrey* (DFL)	884,168	57.5
	P. K. Peterson (Rep.)	648,586	42.2
1964	*Eugene J. McCarthy* (DFL)	931,353	60.3
	Wheelock Whitney (Rep.)	605,933	39.3
1966	*Walter F. Mondale* (DFL)	685,840	53.9
	Robert A. Forsythe (Rep.)	574,868	45.2

Table III. Major Party Vote for Governor in Minnesota, 1920–1966 [a]

Year	Candidate and Party	Votes Cast	Percentage of Total
1920	*J. A. O. Preus* (Rep.)	415,805	53.1
	Henrik Shipstead (FL)	281,402	35.9
	L. C. Hodgson (Dem.)	81,293	10.4
1922	*J. A. O. Preus* (Rep.)	309,756	45.2
	Magnus Johnson (FL)	295,479	43.1
	Edward Indrehus (Dem.)	79,903	11.6
1924	*Theodore Christianson* (Rep.)	406,692	48.7
	Floyd B. Olson (FL)	366,029	43.8
	Carlos Avery (Dem.)	49,353	5.9
1926	*Theodore Christianson* (Rep.)	395,779	56.5
	Magnus Johnson (FL)	266,845	38.1
	Alfred Jaques (Dem.)	38,008	5.4
1928	*Theodore Christianson* (Rep.)	549,857	55.0
	Ernest Lundeen (FL)	227,193	22.7
	Andrew Nelson (Dem.)	213,734	21.4
1930	*Floyd B. Olson* (FL)	473,154	59.3
	Ray P. Chase (Rep.)	289,528	36.3
1932	*Floyd B. Olson* (FL)	522,438	50.6
	Earle Brown (Rep.)	334,081	32.3
	John E. Regan (Dem.)	169,859	16.4
1934	*Floyd B. Olson* (FL)	468,812	44.6
	Martin A. Nelson (Rep.)	396,359	37.7
	John E. Regan (Dem.)	176,928	16.8
1936	*Elmer A. Benson* (FL)	680,342	60.7
	Martin A. Nelson (Rep.)	431,841	38.6
1938	*Harold E. Stassen* (Rep.)	678,839	59.9
	Elmer A. Benson (FL)	387,263	34.2
	Thomas Gallagher (Dem.)	65,875	5.8
1940	*Harold E. Stassen* (Rep.)	654,686	52.1
	Hjalmar Petersen (FL)	459,609	36.5
	Ed Murphy (Dem.)	140,021	11.1
1942	*Harold E. Stassen* (Rep.)	409,800	51.6
	Hjalmar Petersen (FL)	299,917	37.8
	John D. Sullivan (Dem.)	75,151	9.5
1944	*Edward J. Thye* (Rep.)	701,185	61.6
	Byron G. Allen (DFL)	430,132	37.8
1946	*Luther W. Youngdahl* (Rep.)	519,067	59.0
	Harold H. Barker (DFL)	349,565	39.7

[a] Votes for candidates of the Industrial Government party, Communist party, Socialist Worker party, and other minor political groups were omitted because of their small number of votes; hence the figures do not total 100 percent.

153

Table III — Continued

Year	Candidate and Party	Votes Cast	Percentage of Total
1948	*Luther W. Youngdahl* (Rep.)	648,572	53.1
	Charles L. Halsted (DFL)	545,766	45.1
1950	*Luther W. Youngdahl* (Rep.)	635,800	60.7
	Harry H. Peterson (DFL)	400,637	38.3
1952	*C. Elmer Anderson* (Rep.)	785,125	55.3
	Orville L. Freeman (DFL)	624,480	44.0
1954	*Orville L. Freeman* (DFL)	607,099	52.7
	C. Elmer Anderson (Rep.)	538,865	46.8
1956	*Orville L. Freeman* (DFL)	731,180	51.4
	Ancher Nelsen (Rep.)	685,196	48.2
1958	*Orville L. Freeman* (DFL)	658,326	56.8
	George MacKinnon (Rep.)	490,731	42.3
1960	*Elmer L. Andersen* (Rep.)	783,813	50.6
	Orville L. Freeman (DFL)	760,934	49.1
1962	*Karl F. Rolvaag* (DFL)	619,842	49.71
	Elmer L. Andersen (Rep.)	619,751	49.70
1966	*Harold LeVander* (Rep.)	680,593	52.6
	Karl F. Rolvaag (DFL)	607,943	46.9

Table IV. Proposed Amendments to the Minnesota Constitution, 1948–1968

No.	Year on Ballot	Provision of Minnesota Constitution to Be Amended	Purpose of Amendment	Adopted or Rejected	Yes Vote	No Vote	Total Vote at General Election	Percentage Yes Is of Total
1	1948	Art. IX, Sec. 5	To provide for a 50-50 apportionment of excise tax on petroleum products	R	534,588	539,224	1,257,804	42.50
2	1948	Art. XIV, Sec. 1	To authorize submission of two or more amendments without requiring voters to vote separately on each amendment	R	319,667	621,523	1,257,804	25.41
3	1948	Art. XIV, Sec. 2	To authorize ⅔ of the legislature to call for a constitutional convention without submitting the question to the voters	R	294,842	641,013	1,257,804	23.44
4	1948	Add Art. XX	To authorize the state to pay a veterans' bonus	A	664,703	420,518	1,257,804	52.85
5	1950	Art. IX, Sec. 1	To authorize diversion of 1% of the proceeds of the occupation mining tax to the Veterans' Compensation Fund	A	594,092	290,870	1,067,967	55.63
6	1950	Art. VIII, Sec. 2, and repealing Art. IV, Sec. 32(b)	To authorize Forestry Management Funds by diverting certain proceeds (25%) from Public Land Trust Fund	R	367,013	465,239	1,067,967	34.37
7	1950	Art. IX, Sec. 5	To provide for a 50%-44%-6% apportionment of the excise tax on petroleum products proceeds	R	420,580	455,346	1,067,967	39.38
8	1952	Art. VIII, Sec. 6	To authorize a change in the investment and loan requirements governing permanent school and university funds	R	604,384	500,490	1,460,326	41.39

Table IV — Continued

No.	Year on Ballot	Provision of Minnesota Constitution to Be Amended	Purpose of Amendment	Adopted or Rejected	Yes Vote	No Vote	Total Vote at General Election	Percentage Yes Is of Total
9........	1952	Art. XIV, adding a new Sec. 3	To provide for a 60% popular majority of voters voting on the question before a new state constitution can be considered legally ratified by the electorate	R	656,618	424,492	1,460,326	44.96
10........	1952	Art. VII, Sec. 1	To clarify who shall be entitled to vote	R	716,670	371,508	1,460,326	49.08
11........	1952	Art. VI, Sec. 7	To permit the legislature to extend probate court jurisdiction by a ⅔ vote	R	646,608	443,005	1,460,326	44.28
12........	1952	Art. XVI, Sec. 3	To provide for a 65%-10%-25% apportionment of the excise tax on motor vehicles proceeds	R	580,316	704,336	1,460,326	39.74
13........	1954	Art. VI, Sec. 7	To permit the legislature to define qualifications and to extend jurisdiction of probate judges by a ⅔ vote	A	610,138	308,888	1,168,101	52.23
14........	1954	Art. X, Sec. 3	To empower the legislature to limit the liability of stockholders of state banks	A	624,611	290,039	1,168,101	53.47
15........	1954	Art. XIV, Sec. 3 (new); Art. IX, Sec. 4 (not to apply)	To provide for a 60% popular vote before a new state constitution can be held ratified and to remove the constitutional bar against members of the legislature serving in a constitutional convention	A	638,818	266,484	1,168,101	54.69

Table IV — Continued

No.	Year on Ballot	Provision of Minnesota Constitution to Be Amended	Purpose of Amendment	Adopted or Rejected	Yes Vote	No Vote	Total Vote at General Election	Percentage Yes Is of Total
16	1954	Art. V, Sec. 4	To permit gubernatorial appointments in case of vacancy in certain offices to run until the end of the term or Jan. 1 and so eliminate the need for election to short terms (Nov. to Jan.)	A	636,237	282,212	1,168,101	54.47
17	1956	Art. VI	To permit the legislature to recognize the judicial power of the state	A	939,957	307,178	1,449,856	65.10
18	1956	New Art. XVI in place of Art. XVI and Art. IX, Sec. 16	To authorize the consolidation of present trunk highway articles and sections, to increase state aid and supervision of public highways, to permit tax of motor vehicles and fuel, and to apportion moneys for highway purposes on the basis of 62%–29%–9% to state and local government highways	A	1,060,063	230,707	1,449,856	78.42
19	1958	Art. IX, Sec. 1A	To authorize the legislature to divert 50% of occupation mining tax proceeds earmarked for education from permanent trust funds to current educational needs	A	1,084,627	209,311	1,449,856	75.12
20	1958	Art. XI and Art. IV, Sec. 33, and repealing Art. IV, Sec. 36	To authorize the legislature to revise and consolidate provisions on local government, home rule, and special laws	A	712,552	309,848	1,178,178	60.48

Table IV — Continued

No.	Year on Ballot	Provision of Minnesota Constitution to Be Amended	Purpose of Amendment	Adopted or Rejected	Yes Vote	No Vote	Total Vote at General Election	Percentage Yes Is of Total
21	1958	Art. V, Secs. 3 and 5	To provide for 4-year terms for state constitutional officers to take effect for terms beginning in 1963	A	641,887	382,505	1,178,173	54.48
22	1958	Art. IV, Sec. 9	To permit members of the legislature to hold certain elective and nonelective state offices	R	576,800	480,112	1,178,178	48.91
23	1960	Art. IV, Secs. 1 and 9	To extend the length of legislative sessions and to set qualifications for legislators and other elected officers	R	768,484	501,429	1,577,509	48.39
24	1960	Art. IV, Sec. 2, and repealing Art. IV, Secs. 23 and 24	To reapportion state house and senate	R	600,797	661,009	1,577,509	38.08
25	1960	Art. V, Sec. 6	To provide for succession to the governorship and for emergency government	A	974,486	305,245	1,577,509	61.77
26	1960	Art. VII, Sec. 1	To change the time of residence in a precinct required in order to qualify to vote in that precinct	A	993,186	302,217	1,577,509	62.95
27	1962	Art. VIII, Secs. 2, 5, and 6	To consolidate the swampland fund and the permanent school fund to make a perpetual fund for payments to local school districts	A	828,880	288,490	1,267,502	65.39

Table IV — Continued

No.	Year on Ballot	Provision of Minnesota Constitution to Be Amended	Purpose of Amendment	Adopted or Rejected	Yes Vote	No Vote	Total Vote at General Election	Percentage Yes Is of Total
28	1962	Art. IX, Secs. 5, 6, and 7, and repealing Art. IX, Sec. 14	To allow the state to incur indebtedness for temporary borrowing for land acquisition and capital improvement	A	728,255	385,723	1,267,502	57.45
29	1962	Art. IV, Sec. 1	To extend the length of legislative sessions from 90 to 120 days	A	706,761	393,538	1,267,502	55.76
30	1964	Add Art. XXI	To forbid repeal or amendment of Chapter 81 of the Laws of 1963 on taxation of taconite plants for a period of 25 years	A	1,272,590	204,183	1,586,173	80.23
31	1964	Art. IV, Secs. 2, 7, 23, 32(b); Art. V, Sec. 4; Art. VII, Sec. 9; and repealing Art. IV, Sec. 26, and Art. VII, Sec. 8	To remove obsolete language from the Constitution	A	1,089,798	254,216	1,586,173	68.70
32	1966	Art. IV, Sec. 9	To allow legislators to run for other offices and to provide a manner in which they may resign	B	575,967	471,427	1,312,288	43.89
33	1968	Same as No. 32	Same as No. 32	A	1,012,235	359,088	1,601,515	63.20
34	1968	Art. V, Sec. 4, and Art. IV, Sec. 11	To allow the legislature three days after adjournment to present bills to the governor and to allow the governor 14 days in which to sign or veto bills passed during the last three days of a session	A	1,044,418	316,916	1,601,515	65.21

Bibliographical Note and Index

A NOTE ON SOURCES AND FURTHER READINGS

For more extensive bibliographical suggestions, see G. Theodore Mitau, *Selected Bibliography of Research in Minnesota Government, Politics, and Public Finance* (St. Paul, 1960; distributed by the Minnesota Historical Society), and Theodore C. Blegen and Theodore L. Nydahl, *Minnesota History: A Guide to Reading and Study* (Minneapolis: University of Minnesota Press, 1960). The *Legislative Manual* (published biennially by the Minnesota secretary of state), often referred to as the "Blue Book," is a source of much pertinent data on state government and elections.

Chapter 1. Party Patterns, Issues, and Leaders

The classic treatise on Minnesota history up to the end of World War I is William Watts Folwell, *A History of Minnesota* (4 vols.; St. Paul: Minnesota Historical Society, 1921–30); an excellent one-volume work is Theodore C. Blegen, *Minnesota: A History of the State* (Minneapolis: University of Minnesota Press, 1963). The quarterly issues of *Minnesota History* provide articles concerning all periods of the state's history. Encyclopedia annuals are good sources for brief summaries of each year's political events in the state. John H. Fenton, *Midwest Politics* (New York: Holt, Rinehart and Winston, 1966), has material on Minnesota.

An authoritative analysis of the development of the Minnesota constitution is presented in William Anderson and Albert J. Lobb, *A History of the Constitution of Minnesota* (Minneapolis: University of Minnesota, 1921). On some recent changes, see G. Theodore Mitau, "Constitutional Change by Amendment: Recommendations of the Minnesota Constitutional Commission in Ten Years' Perspective," *Minnesota Law Review*, 44:461 (1960).

Midwest protest movements and the story of the Nonpartisan League are thoroughly examined in John D. Hicks, *The Populist Revolt* (Minneapolis: University of Minnesota Press, 1931); Theodore Saloutos and John D. Hicks, *Agricultural Discontent in the Middle West, 1900–1939* (Madison: University of Wisconsin Press, 1951); and Robert L. Morlan, *Political Prairie Fire: The Nonpartisan League, 1915–1922* (Minneapolis: University of Minnesota Press, 1955). Two unpublished Ph.D. theses, prepared at the University of Minnesota, provide analyses of the Farmer-Labor party and Stassen Republicanism: Arthur Naftalin, "The Farmer Labor Party in Minnesota" (1945); and Ivan Hinderaker, "Harold Stassen and Developments in the Republican Party in Minnesota, 1937–1943" (1949). On one aspect of DFL history, see G. Theodore Mitau, "The Democratic-Farmer-Labor Party Schism of 1948," *Minnesota History*,

34:187–94 (Spring 1955). The platforms of Minnesota political parties (1849–1938) were graciously made available to me by Theodore C. Blegen from his collection. The elections of 1962 and 1966 are the subject, respectively, of Ronald Stinnett and Charles H. Backstrom, *Recount* (Washington, D.C.: National Document Publisher, 1964), and David Lebedoff, *The 21st Ballot: A Political Party Struggle in Minnesota* (Minneapolis: University of Minnesota Press, 1969).

There are some excellent works on Minnesota governors: George M. Stephenson, *John Lind of Minnesota* (Minneapolis: University of Minnesota Press, 1935); George H. Mayer, *The Political Career of Floyd B. Olson* (Minneapolis: University of Minnesota Press, 1951); Winifred G. Helmes, *John A. Johnson: The People's Governor* (Minneapolis: University of Minnesota Press, 1949); Robert Esbjornson, *A Christian in Politics: Luther W. Youngdahl* (Minneapolis: T. S. Denison Co., 1955). Harold E. Stassen has outlined his own position in *Where I Stand* (Garden City, N.Y.: Doubleday and Co., 1947). Articles on nineteenth-century protest leaders have appeared in *Minnesota History*: Donald F. Warner, "Prelude to Populism," 32:129–46 (September 1951); Carl H. Chrislock, "Sidney M. Owen, an Editor in Politics," 36:109–26 (December 1958); Martin Ridge, "Ignatius Donnelly, Minnesota Congressman, 1863–69," 36:173–83 (March 1959). Michael Amrine's *This Is Humphrey: The Story of a Senator* (Garden City, N.Y.: Doubleday and Co., 1960), and Winthrop Griffith, *Humphrey: A Candid Biography* (New York: William Morrow, 1965), are campaign biographies. Eugene J. McCarthy gives his account of the 1968 campaign in *The Year of the People* (Garden City, N.Y.: Doubleday and Co., 1969). See also Roger Kennedy, *Men on the Moving Frontier* (Palo Alto, Calif.: American West Publishing Company, 1969), pp. 103–52.

Chapter 2. Election Law and Party Organization

An excellent publication is *A Digest of Minnesota Election Laws* (Minneapolis: Minnesota League of Women Voters, 1967). Some details on local election dates and procedures are given in Floyd O. Flom and Luther J. Pickrel, *In a Democracy Politics Is Your Job*, Public Affairs Series, University of Minnesota Agricultural Extension Service Pamphlet 201 (1958). On the direct primary, see Clarence C. Hein, "The Operation of the Direct Primary in Minnesota: Nominations for State-Wide and Congressional Office" (Ph.D. thesis, University of Minnesota, 1956). On the legal status of political parties, see G. Theodore Mitau, "The Status of Political Party Organization in Minnesota Law," *Minnesota Law Review*, 40:561–79 (April 1956), and "Judicial Determination of Political Party Organizational Autonomy," *Minnesota Law Review*, 42:245 (1958). On various aspects of campaign financing, see Elston E. Roady, "Florida's New Campaign Expense Laws and the Democratic Gubernatorial Primaries," *American Political Science Review*, 48:465–76 (June 1954); G. Theodore Mitau, "Selected Aspects of Centralized and Decentralized Control over Campaign Finance: A Commentary on S 636," *University of Chicago Law Review*, 23:620–29 (Summer 1956); "Campaign Expenditures Limitation of Minnesota Corrupt Practices Act," *Minnesota Law Review*, 40:156 (1956); John C. Obert, "Money, Politics and the Minnesota Story," *Nieman Reports* (Cambridge, Mass.: Harvard University, October 1957). The latter gives an account of the Alexandria experiment. On the 1962 election, see Louise Kuderling, "Recount Uncovers Problems in Election Procedures," *Minnesota Municipalities*, 48:76–78 (March 1963).

Chapter 3. A Partisan Nonpartisan Legislature

On the nonpartisanship issue, see Charles R. Adrian, "The Origins of Minnesota's Non-Partisan Legislature," *Minnesota History,* 33:155–64 (Winter 1952), and "The Non-Partisan Legislature in Minnesota" (Ph.D. thesis, University of Minnesota, 1950); Ralph S. Fjelstad, "How about Party Labels?" *National Municipal Review,* 44:359–64 (July 1955); Arthur Naftalin, "The Failure of the Farmer-Labor Party to Capture Control of the Minnesota Legislature," *American Political Science Review,* 38:71–78 (February 1944).

On state legislators see William P. Tucker, "Characteristics of State Legislators," *Social Science,* 30:94–98 (April 1955), and a series of articles by Wallace Mitchell which ran in the *Minneapolis Star* from November 26, 1958, through January 6, 1959. The *Legislative Manual* has data on legislators for each session.

Chapter 4. Lobbies before the Legislature

I should like to acknowledge gratefully the aid given me in connection with this chapter by Prof. Floyd O. Flom of the University of Minnesota, who made available a number of interview case studies prepared by students in his course on state government.

Various publications of interest groups themselves provide statements of aims and data. League of Women Voters: *Facts* (Washington, D.C.: League of Women Voters of the United States, 1969). The Minnesota Association of Commerce and Industry: *Greater Minnesota* (St. Paul). Labor groups: among the most comprehensive of the legislative reports issued by the various groups are "Biennial Reports," published by the Railroad Brotherhoods Legislative Board, and "Legislative Report," published by the Minnesota AFL-CIO Federation of Labor. Farm groups: *This Is Farm Bureau* (Chicago: American Farm Bureau Federation, 1968); "Farm Bureau: A Short History of the Minnesota Farm Bureau and American Farm Bureau Organization" (St. Paul: Minnesota Farm Bureau, 1968); "Farmers Union 1969 Target Program," adopted by delegates to the 67th Annual Convention of the National Farmers Union, Hot Springs, Ark.; "Farmers Union Facts Sheets," published periodically. Minnesota Education Association: *Minnesota Journal of Education* (St. Paul).

The report of the Governor's Committee on Ethics in Government was issued in St. Paul in January 1959.

INDEX